AF606863

DIES IRÆ

Ecce venit cum nubibus, et videbit eum omnis
oculus, et qui eum pupugerunt.

Behold, He cometh with the clouds, and every eye
shall see Him, even those that pierced Him.

–Apocalypse 1:7

DIES IRÆ

The Sequence of the Mass for the Dead

Dogmatically and ascetically interpreted for devotional reading and meditation by

THE REV. NICHOLAUS GIHR, D.D.

translated from the fourth German edition by

THE REV. JOSEPH J. SCHMIT

BENEDICTUS BOOKS
Manchester, NH

BENEDICTUS
BOOKS

Dies Iræ was originally published in 1927 by B. Herder Book Co., St. Louis. This 2021 edition by Benedictus Books® prefers fidelity to that edition over modernized diction, and so contains only minimal formatting and editorial changes not affecting the original content or style. Citations have been added or amended where necessary.

Approbations from the original:
Nihil obstat: Joannes Rothensteiner, *Censor Librorum*
Imprimatur: Joannes J. Glennon, *Archiepiscopus*
St. Louis, February 17, 1927

Scripture references follow the Douay-Rheims Bible, per the imprint of John Murphy Company (Baltimore, 1899).

Cover by Perceptions Studio
Interior illustration, *The Last Judgment* from the Small Passion by Albrecht Dürer (1511), added from the public domain.

Benedictus Books
Box 5284, Manchester, NH 03108
1-800-888-9344

www.PrayBenedictus.com

ISBN 978-1-64413-572-3

eBook ISBN 978-1-64413-573-0

Library of Congress Control Number: 2021947844

CONTENTS

SCRIPTURE CITATIONS ABBREVIATIONS

Abbr	Douay-Rheims	Contemporary
1 Cor	1 Corinthians	1 Corinthians
1 Esd	1 Esdras	Ezra
1 Jn	1 John	1 John
1 Kgs	1 Kings	1 Samuel
1 Mc	1 Machabees	1 Maccabees
1 Par	1 Paralipomenon	1 Chronicles
1 Pt	1 Peter	1 Peter
1 Thes	1 Thessalonians	1 Thessalonians
1 Tm	1 Timothy	1 Timothy
2 Cor	2 Corinthians	2 Corinthians
2 Esd	2 Esdras (Nehemiah)	Nehemiah
2 Jn	2 John	2 John
2 Kgs	2 Kings	2 Samuel
2 Mc	2 Machabees	2 Maccabees
2 Par	2 Paralipomenon	2 Chronicles
2 Pt	2 Peter	2 Peter
2 Thes	2 Thessalonians	2 Thessalonians
2 Tm	2 Timothy	2 Timothy
3 Jn	3 John	3 John
3 Kgs	3 Kings	1 Kings
4 Kgs	4 Kings	2 Kings
Abd	Abdias	Obadiah
Acts	Acts of the Apostles	Acts of the Apostles
Agg	Aggeus	Haggai
Am	Amos	Amos
Apoc	Apocalypse	Revelation
Bar	Baruch	Baruch
Cant	Canticle of Canticles	Song of Songs
Col	Colossians	Colossians
Dn	Daniel	Daniel
Dt	Deuteronomy	Deuteronomy
Eccles	Ecclesiastes	Ecclesiastes
Ecclus	Ecclesiasticus	Sirach
Eph	Ephesians	Ephesians
Est	Esther	Esther

Abbr	Douay-Rheims	Contemporary
Ex	Exodus	Exodus
Ez	Ezechiel	Ezekiel
Gal	Galatians	Galatians
Gn	Genesis	Genesis
Hb	Habacuc	Habbakuk
Heb	Hebrews	Hebrews
Is	Isaias	Isaiah
Jas	James	James
Jer	Jeremias	Jeremiah
Jb	Job	Job
Jl	Joel	Joel
Jn	John	John
Jon	Jonas	Jonas
Jo	Josue	Joshua
Jude	Jude	Jude
Jgs	Judges	Judges
Jdt	Judith	Judith
Lam	Lamentations	Lamentations
Lv	Leviticus	Leviticus
Lk	Luke	Luke
Mal	Malachias	Malachi
Mk	Mark	Mark
Mt	Matthew	Matthew
Mi	Micheas	Micah
Na	Nahum	Nahum
Nm	Numbers	Numbers
Os	Osee	Hosea
Phlm	Philemon	Philemon
Phil	Philippians	Philippians
Prv	Proverbs	Proverbs
Ps	Psalms	Psalms
Rom	Romans	Romans
Ru	Ruth	Ruth
Soph	Sophonias	Zephaniah
Ti	Titus	Titus
Tb	Tobias	Tobit
Ws	Wisdom	Wisdom
Zac	Zacharias	Zechariah

PUBLISHER'S PREFACE

Msgr. Nicholaus Gihr (1839–1924), a scholar and priest of the Archdiocese of Freiburg, was regarded as one of the most outstanding German liturgists and dogmatic theologians of his time. Contemporary to the great French liturgist Dom Prosper Guéranger, Gihr's monumental work *The Holy Sacrifice of the Mass* (1877) would have similarly far-reaching influence on the theological discourse of several pontificates, including those of Bl. Pius IX, St. Pius X, Benedict XV, and Pius XI.

Gihr's dogmatic and ascetical commentary on the *Dies Iræ*, that greatest and most poetic of all Sequences in the classical Roman Rite, was first published in Freiburg at the turn of the twentieth century (Herder: 1900), and exhibits the same degree of expansive scholarship and depth of insight found in his magnum opus; his theological precision is here blended with a spirit of profound unction, allowing the reader an extended meditation on the *Dies Iræ* that is as informative as it is moving.

The author's mastery of ancient languages and impressive command of primary source material makes for a highly readable text, if it does challenge the conventions of source citation at times. In this new edition of Gihr's book for the benefit of readers in English, we have added translations of several Latin quotations, and expanded annotations whenever possible. Where original references are obscure, we have simply reproduced these without alteration.

DIES IRÆ

I

Introduction

The Franciscan Thomas of Celano (a village in the Abruzzi), who lived and labored in the first half of the thirteenth century (about 1200–1255), was a companion and the first biographer of St. Francis of Assisi. The now almost universally accepted tradition that this Franciscan was the author of the *Dies Iræ* is based upon the testimony of a certain Bartholomew of Pisa, who, in 1385, wrote a book entitled: *Liber Conformitatum S. Francisci cum vita Domini Nostri Iesu Christi.* We read there that Fr. Thomas is reputed to be the author of the Sequence *Dies Iræ*, which is sung in Masses for the dead.[1] We shall have to accept this account in view of the fact that later references to other authors are entirely groundless.

The *Dies Iræ* has come down to us in three different versions or redactions, and the question which was the original text cannot be satisfactorily answered. The shortest text is that of the *Missale Romanum*; both of the other redactions have added several stanzas, the one at the beginning, the other at the end of the poem. The last two stanzas, or the last six lines of our liturgical text, are evidently not the work of the author but must be ascribed to a later date, when the *Dies Iræ* was used as a Mass Sequence. Stanzas 1–6 contain a short but forcible and gripping description of the Last Judgment; stanza 7 is transitional, asking the question: "To whom shall I look for help on this momentous occasion?" There is but one answer possible, and this is given in the extended and deeply earnest prayer of stanzas 8–17. The entire prayer is recited in the first person and grows ever more fervent and penetrating by a beautiful gradation of thought and emotion, until it reaches the words: *Gere curam mei finis*. Here we note an abrupt stop—a strange voice, quite different from that of the trembling and agitated petitioner, continues: "Truly, it is a mournful day, etc." The petitioner seems suddenly to have forgotten about himself; without any apparent reason he no longer prays for himself, but for another.[2]

Like the *Stabat Mater*, the *Dies Iræ* was originally intended for private devotion—a sort of pious meditation on the Last Judgment, whose appeal lay in the graphic portrayal of the emotions that fill the soul of man when, conscious of his guilt, he is reminded of the all-knowing and just Judge. Its excellence caused its adoption as a Sequence in the Mass for the Dead as early as the second half of the fourteenth century, but it was not until the sixteenth century that its use became universal through a rubric of the *Missale Romanum* as revised by Pius V.

The poem is written in rhyming trochaic stanzas, each stanza containing three lines or verses, rendered remarkably forcible by the frequent use of full tones for the endings. A very pleasing effect is produced by the interchange of the closed vowels (*o*, *u*) and the open vowels (*a*, *e*, *i*). After the seventeenth stanza there is a marked change in the construction of the verses. The three concluding stanzas consist of two lines each, ending in imperfect rhymes of one syllable, while all of the preceding rhymes are trochaic.

18. a. *Lacrimosa dies illa*
Qua resurget ex favilla
18. b. *Iudicandus homo reus:*
Huic ergo parce Deus.
19. *Pie Iesu Domine*
Dona eis requiem.

The quiet, earnest, and solemn character of the trochaic verse is admirably adapted for a forcible presentation of the sublime subject treated. While the first and shorter part of the poem (stanzas 1–7) fills the soul with holy fear and consternation by its graphic description of the end of the world and the judgment that is to follow, the second and longer part (stanzas 7–19) portrays in a spirited and gripping fashion the emotions which a serious meditation on the Last Judgment will invariably awaken in a sinful and sorrowful soul. These emotions manifest themselves (stanzas 7–17) in a pathetic plea for pardon, first for the individual and finally (stanzas 18–19) for all the faithful departed. In the liturgical funeral services the so-called "satisfactory fruits" of such prayers and meditations are applied to the deceased persons for whom they are offered. Throughout the entire ceremony, which for perfection in form and sublimity in thought is not surpassed anywhere, the celebrant speaks and acts as if he were standing in the very place of the departed. Similarly, too, in this Sequence the pleas for mercy appear to proceed from the soul of the deceased (*ex anima defuncti*).

The high poetic worth of the *Dies Iræ* (which has been styled "a musical gem even without the music" and "the giant among hymns") is universally recognized and admired even by Protestants. "The Founder of the Franciscan Order," says Professor Thode, "was the pioneer and leader of his followers in the composition of songs of praise. He was followed by Thomas of Celano, who, though he wrote in Latin, seems to have spoken from the very heart of the people, and who is said to have composed that powerful, storm-tossed 'Dies iræ, dies illa,' that touching voice of warning, whose deep tones strangely resemble the mournful accents of the bells."[3] "This musical poem, so sublime, so elevating, so fertile in thought, even though it is altogether untranslatable, has yet tempted many to try their hand at metrical translations and poetical imitations."[4] There are at present more than one hundred translations of this poem into German alone, and many into English, which fact is perhaps the best proof that this Sequence cannot be perfectly reproduced in any other language.

ENDNOTES

1 *Prosam de mortuis, quæ cantatur in Missa, Dies Iræ, dies illa, dicitur fecisse.*

2 P. Dreves.

3 Thode, *Franz von Assisi und die Anfänge der Kunst der Renaissance in Italien*, Berlin, 1885.

4 Koch in Herzog's *Real-Encyclopädie für protestantische Theologie und Kirche, s. v. Dies iræ.*

II

The Text of the Sequence

1

Dies iræ, dies illa:
Solvet sæclum in favilla
Teste David cum Sibylla.

That day of wrath, that dreadful day,
When Heaven and earth shall pass away,
Both David and the Sibyl say.

2

Quantus tremor est futurus,
Quando iudex est venturus,
Cuncta stricte discussurus!

What terror then shall us befall,
When lo, the Judge's steps appall,
About to sift the deeds of all.

3

Tuba mirum spargens sonum
per sepulchra regionum,
Coget omnes ante thronum.

The mighty trumpet's marvellous tone
Shall pierce through each sepulchral stone
And summon all before the throne.

4

Mors stupebit et natura
Cum resurget creatura
Iudicanti responsura.

Now Death and Nature in amaze
Behold the Lord His creatures raise,
To meet the Judge's awful gaze.

5

Liber scriptus proferetur,
In quo totum continetur,
Unde mundus iudicetur.

The books are opened, that the dead
May have their doom from what is read,
The record of our conscience dread.

6

Iudex ergo cum sedebit,
Quidquid latet, apparebit:
Nil inultum remanebit.

The Lord of judgment sits Him down,
And every secret thing makes known;
No crime escapes His vengeful frown.

7

Quid sum, miser, tunc
dicturus,
Quem patronum rogaturus,
Cum vix iustus sit securus?

Ah, how shall I that day endure?
What patron's friendly voice secure,
When scarce the just themselves are
sure?

8

Rex tremendæ maiestatis,
Qui salvandos salvas gratis,
Salva me, fons pietatis.

O King of dreadful majesty,
Who grantest grace and mercy free,
Grant mercy now and grace to me.

9

Recordare, Iesu pie,
Quod sum causa tuæ viæ:
Ne me perdas illa die!

Good Lord, 'twas for my sinful sake,
That Thou our suffering flesh didst take,
Then do not now my soul forsake.

10

Quærens me, sedisti lassus,
Redemisti crucem passus:
Tantus labor non sit cassus!

In weariness Thy sheep was sought;
Upon the Cross his life was bought;
Alas, if all in vain were wrought.

11

Iuste iudex ultionis,
Donum fac remissionis
Ante diem rationis.

O just avenging Judge, I pray,
For pity take my sins away,
Before the great accounting-day.

12

Ingemisco tamquam reus,
Culpa rubet vultus meus:
Supplicanti parce Deus.

I groan beneath the guilt, which Thou
Canst read upon my blushing brow;
But spare, O God, Thy suppliant now.

13

Qui Mariam absolvisti	Thou Who didst Mary's sins unbind
Et latronem exaudisti,	And mercy for the robber find,
Mihi quoque spem dedisti.	Dost fill with hope my anxious mind.

14

Preces meæ non sunt dignæ,	My feeble prayers can make no claim,
Sed tu bonus fac benigne,	Yet gracious Lord, for Thy great name,
Ne perenni cremer igne.	Redeem me from the quenchless flame.

15

Inter oves locum præsta	At Thy right hand, give me a place
Et ab hœdis me sequestra,	Among Thy sheep, a child of grace,
Statuens in parte dextra.	Far from the goats' accursed race.

16

Confutatis maledictis,	Yea, when Thy justly kindled ire
Flammis acribus addictis,	Shall sinners hurl to endless fire,
Voca me cum benedictis.	Oh, call me to Thy chosen choir.

17

Oro supplex et acclinis,	In suppliant prayer I prostrate bend,
Cor contritum quasi cinis:	My contrite heart like ashes rend,
Gere curam mei finis.	Regard, O Lord my latter end.

18

Lacrimosa dies illa,	Oh, on that day, that tearful day,
Qua resurget ex favilla	When man to judgment wakes from clay,
Iudicandus homo reus:	Be Thou the trembling sinner's stay,

19

Huic ergo parce Deus.	And spare him, God, we humbly pray.
Pie Iesu Domine,	Yea, grant to all, O Savior blest,
Dona eis requiem. Amen.	Who die in Thee, the saints' sweet rest. Amen.

We are indebted for the above translation to that scholarly commentary on "The Hymns of the Breviary and Missal" by the Rev. Matthew Britt, O. S. B. Those who are interested in the history of the various translations of the *Dies Iræ* into English, should read Father Britt's exhaustive study of this noble hymn, for apparently he has read every worthwhile translation into English that has appeared to the present time. "It is freely acknowledged," he says, "that no adequate translation has yet appeared." We reproduce from this work the *apologia* of Dr. Coles, a Newark physician, who made eighteen translations of the *Dies Iræ*, and yet maintains that no single version can reflect the totality of the original. "To preserve, in connection with the utmost fidelity and strictness of rendering, all the rhythmic merits of the Latin original—to attain to a vital likeness as well as to an exact literalness, at the same time that nothing is sacrificed of its musical sonorousness and billowy grandeur, easy and graceful in its swing as the ocean in its bed—to make the verbal copy, otherwise cold and dead, glow with the fire of lyric passion—to reflect, and that too by means of a single version, the manifold aspects of the many-sided original, exhausting at once its wonderful fullness and pregnancy—to cause the white light of the primitive so to pass through the medium of another language as that it shall undergo no refraction whatever—would be desirable, certainly, were it practicable; but so much as this it were unreasonable to expect in a single version."[1]

ENDNOTES

1 *The Dies Iræ in Thirteen Original Versions,* p. 33. Editor's Note: For a more literal rendering of the original Latin, see the appendix on p. 113.

III

Interpretation

The story of creation is not the story of an endless series of recurrent changes, nor an eternal process of development and progress. The world, as we know it, will come to an end; the curtain will fall at last upon the historical drama of man and the world in which he lives. The end of the world, "the end of all things" (see 1 Pt 4:7, *πάντων τὸ τέλος*; *omnium finis*) which is to be accompanied by an extraordinary manifestation of divine omnipotence, by no means includes the annihilation of matter, but merely marks the transition of the world to the final *consummatio sæculi* predicted by Jesus Christ (Mt 28:20). This consummation consists in an elevation of the creature to a higher degree of existence, in the supernatural renewal and transfiguration of the whole universe. "For the expectation of the creature waiteth for the revelation of the sons of God. For the creature was made subject to vanity [*vanitati,* i.e. to instability and corruption] not willingly, but by reason of him that made it subject, in hope: because the creature also itself shall be delivered from the servitude of corruption, into the liberty of the glory of the children of God" (Rom 8:19–21). At present, St. Paul says, "every creature groaneth and travaileth in pain" (Rom 8:22) and longs for its deliverance, which will come when it shall participate in the glorious destiny of the elect—of the risen, transfigured children of God.

The momentous events that will accompany the change in creation from time to eternity, from the present unstable order of nature to the lasting and unchangeable order of eternity, are in biblical parlance called "the last things" (see Ecclus 7:40, *τά ἔσχατα*; *novissima*).

For us, these things are of the future, and to obtain some knowledge of them we are forced to rely upon divine revelation, since human reason is altogether inadequate. In revelation we have a fruitful source of information concerning "the last things," but mostly clothed in prophetic and apocalyptic language, so that it is impossible to answer many questions with certainty. The mysterious veil that hides from our view the final stages of the world's history is, evidently, in the providence of God, not yet to be lifted; the light which revelation spreads over them is but a sort of *twilight,* until the day when our faith changes to vision and we shall see God face to face.

St. Augustine frequently mentions the incomplete and unsatisfactory character of our knowledge in discussing eschatological questions: "The prophetic manner of speech loves to mix figures with words that are to be taken in the strictly literal sense (*propriis verbis translata miscere*), so that the real meaning is often, as it were, obscured (*sic quodam modo velare quod dicitur*)."[1]

Just what will happen at the end of the world we shall be able to know adequately only when it actually happens; for the present, we must be content with guesses and conjectures. That the events foretold in Holy Scripture (persecution of the faithful by the antichrist, appearance of the Judge, resurrection of the dead, separation of the good from the wicked, destruction and renewal of the world) will actually happen, we must believe: but their sequence and the manner of happening can only be known from experience; human intelligence cannot fathom the mystery.[2]

The *Dies Iræ* rests upon a biblical foundation. The contents of the Sequence are taken mainly from the prophetical descriptions of the Old Testament, from the eschatological sermons of Christ, and from the teaching and the references of the apostles concerning the consummation of the world. The description of Christ's return as Judge of the universe is in full harmony with Holy Scripture, especially the letters of the apostles. The *time when the end of the world will come* is, and will ever remain, a sealed mystery to angels and men. Even the Divine Master refused to answer the question when put by His apostles (see Mt 24:36), but admonished them to be watchful and ready at any time to render an account of themselves, as the Son of Man would come suddenly and unexpectedly. Because of these repeated warnings of their Divine Master, the apostles very properly believed it *possible* that the Second Coming of Christ, and with it the end of the world, might take place within their own lifetime. "Watch ye, therefore, because you know not the day nor the hour" (Mt 25:13). "Watch ye, therefore, praying at all times, that you may be accounted worthy to escape all these things that are to come, and to stand before the Son of Man" (Lk 21:36). "It is not for you to know the times or moments, which the Father hath put in his own power" (Acts 1:7).

Since the Messianic or Christian era, referred to by St. Peter as "the last times" (1 Pt 1:20), marks the beginning of the closing period of the world's history, the Second Coming of Christ as Judge may occur at any time, and in this sense it is ever near at hand. Therefore the apostles frequently dwelt upon Christ's Second Coming, and particularly during the early days of suffering and persecution, this thought was a source of comfort as well as a means of strengthening their confidence and encouraging them to persevere in following Christ. In a similar way, the Second Coming of Christ is presented for our meditation in the *Dies Iræ.* As indicated in the seventh stanza, the author pictures the Day of Judgment not as far off but as near at hand, and in spirit assumes the position of a living witness at the dread moment when the Judge makes His unexpected appearance.

This view-point appears all the more justified since the particular judgment takes place immediately after the death of every man, and the general judgment at the end of the world is but a solemn ratification and promulgation of the judgment passed at death. Even though centuries may elapse before the end of the world becomes a reality for all mankind, for the individual it becomes a reality at his or her *death.* Therefore, whatever is said of the end of the world and the general judgment, must, in part at least, be applied to *death* and the *particular judgment.* We must bear this in mind for a proper understanding of the biblical and liturgical texts, because both the Bible and the liturgy stress the general judgment at the end of the world much more frequently and impressively than the particular judgment at the end of human life, though the latter is never excluded from, but usually included in, the former. "Among the many things which we are anxious to know," says St. John Chrysostom, "stands first and foremost the time when the end of the world will take place. Nor is it surprising that we should desire to know this, since even the apostles were curious in regard to it. They questioned the Master about it both during His public ministry and after His Resurrection. But later, when the Holy Ghost had enlightened them, this uncertainty and ignorance was of minor concern to them—in fact we find them taking issue with those who busied themselves with such untimely and unnecessary subtleties (see 1 Thes 5:1–2). What would it profit us to know the time of the Judgment Day? Assuming that the end of the world were to come in ten, twenty, thirty, or a hundred years; would it benefit us to know it? Is not the end of his own life the last day for every man? Instead of laboring zealously for our own salvation, therefore, we are wasting time if we indulge in vain speculations concerning the end of the world. See to it that thy own life will end happily, and the end of the world will hold no terrors for thee, and it will matter little to thee whether it be near or far away. There is a close relationship between the death of the individual and the end of the world. What happens to the individual at death, will happen to the whole human race when the world will come to an end. It would not be amiss, therefore, to speak of the death of an individual as that individual's last day or end of the world."[3]

We are, therefore, admonished in the *Dies Iræ* never to lose sight of the return of Christ as Judge (both at death and at the end of the world) and to consider His coming as ever near at hand. Our entire life should be an Advent—a period of expectation and preparation for death and judgment. We should always look forward eagerly to the day when the Savior will come back in the fullness of His power to judge mankind and to bring His Kingdom to a glorious consummation.

It is from this point of view and in this spirit that we should recite and meditate upon the Sequence of the Dead, so that it may produce its full effect upon our minds and hearts.

THE FIRST STANZA

Of all the portentous events that shall mark the end of time, the author of the *Dies Iræ* has singled out what is generally accepted as the most dreadful and terrifying—namely, the destruction of the universe by fire.

DIES IRÆ

Dies iræ, dies illa:
Solvet sæclum in favilla
Teste David cum Sibylla.

"A day of wrath is that day, which will destroy the world and turn it into ashes, as David and the Sibyl testify."

In this first verse of our hymn, the Last Day is briefly described as a dreadful day of wrath, and this particular phrase is undoubtedly chosen in order to fill the hearts of the guilty sinner with fear and trembling. Holy Scripture designates the Christian era in which we live as "the last times" (1 Pt 1:20), "the last hour" (1 Jn 2:18), and "the end of ages" (Heb 9:26), because no other era is to follow the final consummation of the Kingdom of God. The end of the world, however, i.e., that particular period that will witness the Second Coming of Christ and the events that are to accompany it, is in a more restricted sense referred to as "the last time" (1 Pt 1:5) and more often as "the Last Day" (Jn 6:39–40; and Jb 19:25; *dies novissimus*), because then indeed will the days of earth be ended, as after the judgment "time shall be no more" (Apoc 10:6; *tempus non erit amplius*), and the day will dawn that hath no night and no end, "the day of eternity" (2 Pt 3:18; see Apoc 22:5).

Holy Scripture contains many expressions that vividly portray the significance of "the Last Day," when those extraordinary events will take place that will fill men with fear and trembling, when Christ will triumph over all His enemies, and God's infinite justice and mercy, His power and omniscience, and His divine providence that rules with infinite wisdom will shine forth in clearest light. For this reason it is called "the great day" (Jude 1:6), "the day of the Lord" (1 Thes 5:2), "the great and manifest day of the Lord" (Acts 2:20), "the great day of the Almighty God" (Apoc 16:14). With emphatic brevity it is called "*the* day," (Heb 10:25; and 1 Cor 3:13), and quite frequently "*that* day" (2 Tm 1:12; 4:8; and Mt 7:22; *ἡ ἡμέρα ἐκείνη*; *illa dies*), i.e., the day of days, the day par excellence, the well-known day of judgment and retribution. We find the scriptural references to "that day" occurring even in passages where the preceding texts contain no reference to the Day of Judgment.

"*That* day," therefore, that is so often and so impressively referred to by the holy men of God inspired by the Holy Ghost (2 Pt 1:21), is here described as "a day of wrath," namely, the day on which the "wrath" of God, which can only mean His infinite justice, will be fully manifested in His judgments upon a sinful world.

"The wrath of God," says St. Augustine, "unlike the wrath of men, is not a passionate outburst of the disturbed irascible temper, but the calm apportionment of a just punishment (*tranquilla justi supplicii constitutio*)."[4] In the prophetic books of the Old Testament, there are frequent metaphorical references to the wrath of God in meting out justice to the sinner. We find the same idea developed in one of the responses (*Libera*) of the Office of the Dead: *Dies illa, dies iræ, calamitis et miseriæ, dies magna et amara valde*; "that day, the day of wrath, is a day of tribulation and distress, truly a great and bitter day." These liturgical texts are adopted from the prophecy of Sophonias, who nearly seven hundred years before Christ predicted the punishment that would come upon Judah and Jerusalem for their crimes. "The great day of the Lord is near, it is near and exceedingly swift; the voice of the day of the Lord is bitter.... That day is a day of wrath, a day of tribulation and distress, a day of calamity and misery, a day of darkness and obscurity, a day of clouds and whirlwinds, a day of the trumpet" (Soph 1:14–16); a "day of the Lord's indignation"; a day of "the fierce anger of the Lord" (Soph 2:2–3; see Jl 2:2; Am 5:20; and Na 2:10).

The particular judgments of God, meted out in the course of centuries to individual lands and peoples, may be looked upon as shadows and types of the general judgment at the end of the world; only in the latter do the former receive their full realization. The *idea* of God's judgment of the human race includes all of the preceding individual judgments as well as the greatest and Last Judgment, sometimes called the universal judgment. This we must bear in mind for a correct understanding of the prophetical visions and descriptions of God's punitive judgment at the end of the world. The inspired prophet *visions* the full content and notion of God's judgment upon the world, and in order to give full expression to this idea, he draws a picture which brings out the striking characteristics of the particular judgments that have gone before as well as of the universal judgment that is yet to come. The latter constitutes not merely a sublime background for the former, but the characteristics of both commingle, and only in their combination do they afford a true and exhaustive image of God's judgment of the world.

Thus the prophet Isaias in his description of the terrible judgment of God upon Babylon—the prototype of the powers of evil arraigned against God—draws a picture identical in line and color with that of the universal judgment. "Behold the day of the Lord shall come, a cruel day, and full of indignation, and of wrath, and fury, to lay the land desolate and to destroy the sinners thereof out of it. For the stars of heaven and their brightness shall not display their light; the sun shall be darkened in his rising, and the moon shall not shine with her light. And I will visit the evils of the world, and against the wicked for their iniquity; and I will make the pride of infidels to cease, and will bring down the arrogancy of the mighty" (Is 13:9–11).

On that day, the wrath of God will be kindled and burn like fire (Ps 2:13; and 88:47); the mercy and goodness of God, so often abused by men, will be ended, and His justice only will rule. Then will He demand of us a strict account of our stewardship. In this world "all the ways [i.e., counsels and directions] of the Lord are mercy and justice" (Ps 24:10), but His *mercy* predominates over His justice as long as the days of earthly probation last. Here below, God manifests chiefly His grace and goodness, His mildness and mercy, His patience and longanimity. *Dominus expectantissimus indicator.*[5] True, even here below, God sometimes judges and punishes individuals as well as nations; but these temporal visitations always presuppose grace, and His justice tempered by mercy leads to the conversion, to the spiritual progress, and often to the salvation of souls. The trials which God sends are not designed "for the destruction, but for the correction and conversion" of men, and hence "it is a token of great goodness when sinners are not suffered to go on in their ways for a long time, but are presently punished" (2 Mc 6:12–13). Therefore, whether God is strict or lenient with us, we ought always to make use of "the acceptable time" (2 Cor 6:2) to work out our salvation.

The delay of Christ's return to judge mankind is but another manifestation of His infinite love. "The Lord delayeth not His promise, as some imagine, but dealeth patiently for your sake, not willing that any should perish, but that all should return to penance" (2 Pt 3:9). We cannot form a holier and more salutary idea of the task of Christianity than by conceiving it as *the continued manifestation of God's mercy to men.* Every day that dawns is a new grace, another proof of God's infinite forbearance. The centuries of time are the waiting of a Father Who is longing to see His children do penance and participate in His glory. God pours out His mercies lavishly upon the children of men, but the individual can avail himself of grace only to the day of his death, and the human race only until the Last Judgment. These are the immovable goal posts of His mercy, and beyond them *justice* alone shall reign.

Through the ungrateful neglect and the rebellious abuse of grace and the means of grace in course of time God's anger is kindled and inflamed more and more, until at last the measure of sins is full, and the final day of reckoning brings the destructive judgment of God upon a godless world. The very richness of God's benevolence and the depth of His mercy give us a faint idea of the terrifying severity of divine justice as exercised on the dread day of reckoning and throughout all eternity. Bearing in mind this "day," on which God, in Christ, "will judge the world in equity," all sinners should without delay do penance for their sins and change their manner of life (Acts 17:30–31). The apostle admonishes the faithful not to receive "the grace of God in vain" as long as "the day of salvation" lasts (2 Cor 6:1–2); for if this day is allowed to pass unused, they are lost. He who hardens his heart and despises the goodness and patience of God "treasures up to himself wrath, against the day of wrath, and revelation of the just judgment of God" (Rom 2:5; *thesaurizat sibi iram in die iræ et revelationis iusti iudicii Dei*). He who refuses to give ear to the universal invitation of a merciful Redeemer and to obey now must bend in submission to the power of an angry Judge when the time of probation and grace has expired. Spare us, O Lord, that from generation to generation we may sing Thy mercy and Thy justice, Thy goodness and Thy judgment!

There is a divinely ordained intimate relationship between *man* and *nature*; in good and evil, in reward and punishment, their interests are common. Through the sin of Adam and Eve, the earth was involved in the curse (*maledicta terra*, Gn 3:17); through the power of the Redemption, the earth with the children of God was freed from the ancient corruption and adorned with the splendor of a supernatural transfiguration. But God must first pass final judgment upon the visible creation: "Let the heavens rejoice, and let the earth be glad ... because He cometh: because He cometh to judge the earth. He shall judge the world (*iudicare terram*) with justice and the people with His truth" (Ps 95:11, 13). The world will be destroyed by fire—it will be judged by fire. Over and over again the Church repeats this truth in her liturgical prayers: *Christus venturus est iudicare vivos et mortuos, et sæculum per ignem.* Fire is, therefore, the means that will be employed by God to judge, punish, and renew things at the consummation of the world. Of all the catastrophes and momentous changes that have ever visited the earth, surely there is none so stupendous as the destruction of the world by fire. This may be gathered from the description which is given of it by the Prince of the Apostles and which forms perhaps the best commentary on that brief passage of our Sequence.

Solvet sæclum in favilla.

St. Peter begins by contrasting the final conflagration with the deluge. The ancient world, as it existed before the deluge, "being overflowed with water, perished. But the heavens and the earth which are now, by the same word are kept in store, reserved unto fire against the Day of Judgment and perdition of the ungodly men" (2 Pt 3:6–7). This future conflagration will be much more terrible and destructive than the deluge. On this Last Day, the heavens shall pass away with the speed of a rushing wind and the mighty roar of a tempest; flames will dissolve the heavens (*cæli ardentes solventur*); the elements, the solid constituents of earth, will melt (*calore solventur*), and in consequence, the whole earth and everything that is in it will be burnt up and destroyed (see 2 Pt 3:10, 12).

The "world" (*sæculum*) that will be consumed by fire on that fatal day is the earth with its immediate atmosphere, not the starry regions of the universe. The heavenly bodies will no doubt be powerfully influenced by this catastrophe, but they will not be destroyed by fire.

The world conflagration will be confined to the earth and its sphere, i.e., to the dwelling-place of men and the scene of their history.

This (presumably volcanic) catastrophe will reduce the world to "dust and ashes" (*solvet in favilla*) but will not annihilate it. Merely the "form" (*σχήμα, figura*), i.e., the present outline, or what St. Paul calls the "fashion of this world," will pass away (1 Cor 7:31). The destructive fire that will break forth from the bowels of the earth as well as descend from the sky will completely envelop this planet and shake its very foundations; it will destroy the works of nature and those of art that the genius of man has produced. From the resultant chaos, the wreckage of confused elements, and the ruins of a destroyed world, the Almighty will reconstruct "new heavens" and "a new earth" (2 Pt 3:13). *Perspicuum est cælum et terram non perire et in nihilum redigi, sed in melius commutari*; "It is clear that Heaven and earth do not perish and are not reduced to nothing, but that they are changed into something better."[6] This "new heaven" and this "new earth" will spring into being, not as the result of a special creative act of God but rather as the result of a clarifying and cleansing process in the reconstruction of the present Heaven and earth, in which process the final conflagration is to play a part.

The principal purpose of the world-conflagration is undoubtedly to cleanse the earth and all earthly things from every species of impurity. For this purpose no element is better suited than fire, for destruction by fire spells purification, inasmuch as fire purges earthly things from whatever impurity may cling to them. There is nothing that can withstand the power and energy of this rarefied element, and therefore fire must be considered as the most drastic and, in consequence, the most admirably fitted means chosen by God to purify the earth from the stain of sin. Devouring flames are the means chosen by the Judge of the world to purify the material creation from its twofold corruption: from rottenness and filth, corruption and decay on the one hand; on the other, from the moral stains, the degradation and desecration through the sins and crimes of men.

By means of this refining process, the material world will be prepared for its supernatural transformation and brought nearer to its final state of perfection. From the glowing embers, there will rise at God's command the new world foretold by the prophet Isaias (65:17). The present heavens and the present earth will enter upon a new state, the state of supernatural transfiguration. This newly perfected and transformed world, immaculately pure, radiantly beautiful, glowing with marvelous light and color, will proclaim for all eternity the glory of the Creator and of the Redeemer and fill with ecstasy and enduring joy the happy mortals who will be privileged to see and inhabit it. "For behold I create new heavens and a new earth; and the former things shall not be in remembrance ... But you shall be glad and rejoice forever in these things which I create ... and the voice of weeping shall no more be heard ... nor the voice of crying" (Is 65:17–19).

Teste David cum Sibylla.

That the Lord shall one day judge the world and purify it by means of the all-consuming, but at the same time, clarifying element of fire is a truth for which we have the testimony of the prophets, which agrees with the traditions current among the pagan nations, so that this dogma may be said to be confirmed by the voice of the whole human race.

The destruction, or rather, the transformation and renewal of the created universe, is to take place at the end of time; for this we have the infallible testimony of the Old Testament prophets. "David" here stands for the prophets in general, and his prophetic utterances shall light our way, shall shine in the dark places of this world until, with the Second Coming of Christ, the day of eternity shall dawn and the morning star of heavenly transformation shall rise in our hearts (see 2 Pt 1:19). "Much concerning the Day of Judgment is said in the Psalms, but most of it is barely hinted at or mentioned in passing."[7] The following passage from the Psalms, however, in St. Augustine's opinion, "treats distinctly and specifically of the judgment": "In the beginning, O Lord, Thou foundedst the earth; and the heavens are the works of Thy hands. They shall *perish*, but Thou remainest [unchanged and unchangeable]; and all of them shall grow old like a garment; and as a vesture Thou shalt change them, and they shall be changed. But Thou art always the selfsame [unchanged], and Thy years shall not fail" (Ps 101:26–28, emphasis added). The prophet Isaias describes the catastrophe in which the universe will literally wither away and disappear at the approach of the angry Judge as follows: "And all the host of the heavens shall pine away, and the heavens shall be folded together as a book; and all their host shall fall down as the leaf falleth from the vine, and from the fig tree.... Lift up your eyes to heaven, and look down to the earth beneath, for the heavens shall vanish like smoke, and the earth shall be worn away [disintegrate into dust and ashes] like a garment, and the inhabitants thereof shall perish in like manner" (Is 34:4; and 51:6).

The testimony of David, the seer and singer of the Old Testament, is corroborated by that of the "Sibyl," a virginal prophetess, who is the medium and mouthpiece of the religious or inspired traditions of paganism. Reference is here made presumably to the Erythrean or to the Samian Sibyl, both of whom were credited with prophecies concerning the Last Judgment and the end of the world. Since the thirteenth century (when the *Dies Iræ* was composed), Christian art has placed the Sibyls at the side of, or rather opposite to, the prophets. The twelve books of Sibylline prophecy that have come down to us are not genuine; they were partly enlarged, partly invented during the first centuries of the Christian era. In the early days of Christianity as well as in the Middle Ages, there was a widespread belief in the genuineness of these prophecies. *Etiam Sibyllæ multa vera prædixerunt de Christo*; "the Sibyls foretold many true things about Christ."[8] "Why should I mention the Erythrean or the Samian or the Cumean or any of the other eight Sibyls—Varro holds that there were ten of them—whose chief distinction was their virginity and who as a reward received the gift of prophecy? In the Aeolian dialect the word 'Sibyl' means 'one inspired by God' (*θεο-βούλη*) and it is justly said that virginity alone shares the counsels of God (*consilium Dei nosse*)."[9] Lactantius quotes the pronouncements of the Sibyls as divinely inspired and therefore as undeniable testimonies. "One of the Sibyls," he says, "has foretold the future conflagration (*deflagrationem postea futurum vaticinata est*), that shall again destroy the godlessness of mankind (as it was once destroyed by the deluge)."[10] St. Augustine quotes an utterance of the so-called Erythrean Sibyl that has reference to the destruction of the world,[11] but he does not attribute any great value to it. In his opinion "it is believed, not without reason," that certain individuals outside of the Chosen People received revelations concerning future mysteries, but he adds that one might readily suppose these prophecies to have been invented by the Christians: *istæ prophetiæ possunt putari a Christianis esse confictæ.*[12]

If we reflect seriously upon the terrible earnestness, the infallibly certain and unexpectedly sudden advent of the great Judgment Day, on which the world with all its pomp and glory will be reduced to smoke and ashes, we shall find in these truths an abundance of powerful motives for leading a more pious, a more devout, a truly Christian life. The Prince of the Apostles employs these truths as moral motives in his exhortations. Now that the end of the world is at hand (see 1 Pt 4:7), and since all that is in the world is perishable and will eventually be dissolved, we must practice with zeal and energy all virtues, so that we may be found unspotted and blameless before our Judge (see 2 Pt 3:11–14). "The world passeth away, and the concupiscence thereof" (1 Jn 2:17). Earthly happiness hath no permanency—it is like a dissolving haze, a vanishing dream. *Lætitia sæculi vanitas. Cum magna expectatione speratur, ut veniat, et non potest teneri cum venerit. Et transeunt omnia et evolant omnia et sicut fumus vanescunt, et væ qui amant talia: omnis enim anima sequitur quod amat*; "The pomp and glory of the world that beckons so enticingly, what is it but vanity? We pursue it with a restless ardor, yet when we think we have caught it, it eludes our grasp. All things pass like smoke into thin air, and woe to those who have set their hearts upon perishable things: for the soul follows that which it loves."[13]

"It is vanity to love things that shortly shall pass away, and not to haste thither where joy is everlasting.... Study, therefore, to withdraw thy heart from the love of visible things, and turn it to the things that are invisible."[14] And yet we cling so foolishly and sinfully to this fleeting, unstable world. *Ecce, talis est mundus et sic amatur. Ruinosa est domus et piget migrare*; "Behold, such is the world, and even so it is loved. The house is in ruins, and we are too lazy to move."[15] The vainglory of the world—*sæculum hoc modo nitens et fulgens in pompis suis*[16]—shall collapse: an ash-heap is all that will remain of its glitter and tinsel and pomp. *Structor mundi dicit tibi ruiturum mundum, et non credis?* "The Creator of the world says the world shall fall, and you do not believe it?"[17] The shortness of life and the nearness of eternity, the perishableness and instability of all that is earthly, ought to spur us on to combat against the secular spirit and the love of the world, and to prompt us to abandon the world before it abandons us. Consider how fleeting and vain, how changeable and corruptible are all the things that live and exist. Whatever enters upon the scene of this world must take its departure; whatever is born is born to die, and all things that exist will inevitably perish. Time, like a restless bird never tiring in its flight, rushes on and on, and whatsoever it touches must needs change and pass away, for in time and through time all things under the sun are changeable. Man is no exception to this law. He is drawn into the vortex of changes; he has not a lasting abode here on earth. "In the morning man shall grow up like grass; in the morning he shall flourish and pass away: in the evening he shall fall, grow dry, and wither" (Ps 89:6; see 1 Pt 1:24). "I have seen all things that are done under the sun, and behold all is vanity and vexation of spirit" (Eccles 1:14). "Man born of a woman, living for a short time, is filled with many miseries. Who cometh forth like a flower, and is destroyed, and fleeth as a shadow, and never continueth in the same state" (Jb 14:1–2). "My spirit shall be wasted, my days shall be shortened, and only the grave remaineth for me" (Jb 17:1). The inspired writer, suggests Geissel, "so vividly portrays the brevity of life in order that man may not be unmindful of Him Who is the Lord and Ruler of life and hath set its bounds and limitations; that he who is tossed about in the mutation of time may not forget Him Who is immutable, that he who is but dust may not set his heart upon the things of earth that are but dust and shall return unto dust."

That this earth will be destroyed by fire and a new earth shall come into being is clearly stated in our Sequence and in Holy Scripture (see 2 Pt 3:10). It is not so clear, however, just what position this catastrophe will occupy in the chain of events that will mark Judgment Day. The question whether it will be the beginning or the end of the series of eschatological occurrences on that day cannot be definitely answered. From the biblical descriptions, we can draw a composite picture of what shall happen at the end of the world, but we cannot with any degree of certainty place the individual events in their exact chronological order. While many theologians teach with St. Thomas that the destruction of the world by fire shall precede the judgment, there are others who hold with St. Augustine that only after the Last Judgment shall the world be destroyed and renewed. Each of these opinions contains a measure of truth, and by combining both we may get nearer to the full truth. Following this plan, we arrange the events in the following order. According to certain indications in Holy Scripture (see Ps 96:3; 17:9; 49:3; and Is 66:15–16), the destructive flames will probably precede the arrival of the Great Judge. The fire is to continue to burn during the judgment and immediately after the verdict will envelop and destroy the whole world. The actual destruction of the world by fire, therefore, will follow the verdict of the Judge. After the Lord has judged "the living and the dead," He will "judge the world by fire" (*sæculum per ignem*).[18] The final renewal and supernatural transfiguration of the created universe is to be the last act of the great drama, for we can scarcely conceive a new Heaven and a new earth, radiant with the beauty and glory of God's justice and sanctity, arising from the ruins of our earth until every vestige of moral filth and corruption has been cleansed away and the reprobate sinners with their malice and impiety have been hurled into hell. Then only will He Who sitteth upon the throne say: "Behold, I make all things new" (Apoc 21:5).

THE SECOND STANZA

We come now to the description of the Last Judgment. This is the central point around which gravitate the various eschatological events that precede and follow. The final judgment will be terrible, and therefore the Day of Judgment is a day of wrath and woe.

Quantus tremor est futurus,
Quando iudex est venturus,
Cuncta stricte discussurus.

The Day of Judgment as well as the judgment itself is here proposed for our meditation as the object and source of fear and trembling (*dies tremenda, tremendum iudicium*). To account for this universal fear, special emphasis is placed upon "the arrival" of the all-knowing and strict Judge. At His glorious arrival, nature will be unwontedly disturbed, and all mankind will be filled with fear and trepidation. In a word, all nature will be affected when final judgment is passed upon the human race. For this we have proof in many passages of Holy Writ. Before the Lord comes, "the earth hath trembled, the heavens are moved: the sun and the moon are darkened, and the stars have withdrawn their shining ... for the day of the Lord is great and very terrible: and who can stand it? ... And I will shew wonders in heaven and in earth, blood, and fire, and vapor of smoke. The sun shall be turned into darkness, and the moon into blood: before the great and dreaded day of the Lord doth come" (Jl 2:10–11, 30–31). "The sun shall be darkened, and the moon shall not give her light, and the stars shall fall from heaven, and the powers of heaven shall be moved" (Mt 24:29). The sidereal heavens will be mightily shaken and light turned into darkness. The heavenly bodies will be wrenched from their orbits and fall dashing to the earth. On the earth itself there will be distress (*pressura*, "great anguish") among the nations, by reason of the roaring of the sea and the waves, which will cause men to wither away for fear, in expectation of what shall come upon the whole world (see Lk 21:25–26). These physical cataclysms, these terrible manifestations of nature will be the work of God's own hand, the certain signs and forebodings of the coming of the Judge. They will usher in the Day of Judgment.

Let us place ourselves in spirit in the midst of this universal confusion, disorder, and destruction, and picture to ourselves, if we can, the darkness and the meteoric falling of the stars from Heaven, and we shall understand why indescribable "dread" and "trembling" (*tremor*) will seize every human being, and many will wither away from fear, in expectation of what shall come upon the world (see Lk 21:26). But these sudden and violent changes, these strange and unnatural phenomena will not be the only reason for fear and trembling. Equally terrifying will be the advent of the Great Judge and the rigor of His judgments. "The Lord will come in the glory of His majesty, and accompanying Him there will be innumerable legions of angels, radiant in their splendor."[19] When He appears, the resurrection of the dead will have taken place. And so wonderful, so strikingly beautiful will be the sudden appearance of the transfigured God-Man Who comes to judge, that not only men, but also the angels will be filled with fear and trembling. The effect on the elect of God and the reprobate souls, however, will be quite different. The good will tremble in holy adoration and ecstasy, for joy and expectation, for now indeed they may "lift up" their heads, as their "redemption is at hand" (Lk 21:28). For them the final triumph, the day of eternal glory is at hand. The sinners, on the other hand, will tremble in fear and anguish, literally overcome by the terrifying sight of the angry Judge Who has come to pass sentence upon them. The despairing fear of the wicked rather than the reverent and joyful exhilaration of the chosen is emphasized in our Sequence, for it insists again and again that the "Day of Judgment" is the day of "perdition of the ungodly men" (2 Pt 3:7).

Quando iudex est venturus.

That Christ will come *again*, i.e., that He will come visibly a second time at the end of the world to judge the living and the dead, is a fundamental truth of our holy faith. The object of His first coming was to redeem sinners; that of His second coming will be to judge men. This terror-inspiring return of Christ as Judge is to be the final act in the work He came to accomplish, and therefore a necessary extension and completion of His first coming as Redeemer. The *merciful Redeemer* will come again, but this time as a stern Judge Who shall demand a reckoning from those whom He has redeemed concerning the proper use they have made of the graces of the Redemption. It is apparent from this connection between the first and the second coming of Christ, that He will be our Judge as man, i.e., according to His human nature, exercising unlimited jurisdiction. The Father "hath given him power to do judgment, because He is the Son of Man" (Jn 5:27), i.e., because He has personally assumed human nature and redeemed mankind. The Father "hath given all judgment to the Son" (Jn 5:22), so that in visible form He might sit in judgment over the visible creation. The same Christ Who suffered and died in infinite self-abasement, but Who also rose gloriously from the dead, "is He Who was appointed by God to be Judge of the living and of the dead" (Acts 10:42). His judicial power and activity is the natural result of His royal dignity and kingly domain, of His undisputed jurisdiction over every creature, in Heaven, on earth, and in hell. In order to exercise the office of judge not only in a true sense, but perfectly, requires wisdom and justice as well as authority. The God-Man possesses the plenitude of power and jurisdiction, since He not only is infinitely holy but "knoweth all things" and "canst do all things" in order "to judge His people with justice, and the poor with judgment" (1 Jn 3:20; Jb 42:2; and Ps 71:2).

Majestic and solemn beyond compare will be the final judgment of the world. The glorious appearance of the Judge, His dignified bearing and solemn execution of judgment will be in perfect accord with the picture which Holy Scripture paints in glowing colors: "The Lord hath reigned, let the earth rejoice: let many islands be glad. Clouds and darkness are round about Him: justice and judgment are the establishment of His throne. A fire shall go before Him and shall burn His enemies round about. His lightnings have shone forth to the world: the earth saw and trembled. The mountains melted like wax at the presence of the Lord: at the presence of the Lord of all the earth. The heavens declared His justice: and all people saw His glory" (Ps 96:1–6). "God shall come manifestly: our God shall come, and shall not keep silence. A fire shall burn before Him: and a mighty tempest shall be round about Him. He shall call heaven from above, and the earth, to judge His people.... And the heavens shall declare His justice: for God is Judge" (Ps 49:3–4, 6). Suddenly, unexpectedly, "as lightning cometh out of the east, and appeareth even into the west" (Mt 24:27), so the Son of Man will appear in the fullness of His dignity as King, in the plenitude of His authority as Judge. We will single out in this connection a few of the details that accentuate the majesty of Christ at His Second Coming:

a) On the Judgment Day itself, immediately before the arrival of the Judge, there "shall appear the sign (*τὸ σημεῖον, signum*) of the Son of Man in heaven" (Mt 24:30), and this will remain in view until the end of the judgment. This sign is none other than the Cross. "The Cross is the true and characteristic sign of Christ. The sign of a luminous cross shall precede the King to announce Him Who was once crucified."[20] Some were of the opinion that the true Cross (*lignum crucis Christi*) on which Christ died would be miraculously restored and carried before Him by angels at His coming. Much more probable, however, is the opinion suggested by certain expressions both in Sacred Scripture and the liturgy of the Church, that there shall appear in the heavens a wondrously dazzling, luminous cross, so placed that all mankind will be attracted by its splendor. Naturally this exalted sign of Christ's triumph will profoundly impress everyone: the "enemies of the Cross of Christ" (Phil 3:18) will cry out for shame and terror, and the "tribes of the earth" will "mourn" (Mt 24:30), while the friends and lovers of the Cross, the patient and persevering followers of Christ Crucified, will be filled with consolation and joyous expectation at the sight of the glorious wounds of the Judge.

b) The return of Christ as Judge is referred to in Holy Scripture as "the revelation of His glory" (1 Pt 4:13; *revelatio gloriæ eius*), as "the coming of the glory" (Ti 2:13; *adventus gloriæ*), and as "the brightness of His coming" (2 Thes 2:8; *illustratio adventus*). At His first coming, He "emptied Himself, taking the form of a servant" (Phil 2:7), to all appearances weak and lowly; but when He returns, He will come "with great power and majesty" (Lk 21:27; cf. *in maiestate sua*, Mt 25:31). Ever since the Ascension, Christ reigns "in the glory of God the Father"; a mysterious veil still hides the splendor of His glory from our sight, but at the end of time, the veil that now conceals Him will be lifted, and He will appear visibly in the light of His glory and manifest Himself as the "King of Glory" to all the world. On Mount Tabor, His "face did shine as the sun" (Mt 17:2); what splendor may we not look for on the Judgment Day, when He will appear with "the body of His glory" (Phil 3:21; *corpus claritatis*), the glory of the risen Savior?

c) It is quite frequently emphasized in Holy Scripture that the Lord shall come "in the clouds of heaven" (Mt 24:30; *in nubibus cæli*) or simply "in a cloud" (Lk 21:27). Dark, dense clouds are an indication of unapproachable majesty and severity and will therefore form an awe-inspiring garment for Jesus Christ when He returns to the earth as Judge. And yet, since His mission is not merely to terrorize sinners and to overthrow His enemies but also to perfect the work of Redemption and bring joy to the hearts of those who love Him, we are free to believe that the clouds which surround Him will have the proverbial "silver lining"—dark and sinister on one side, they will be bright on the other. It is true that the Redeemer in His clarified body needs no support; therefore, He is said to float above or between "the clouds of heaven" that envelop Him like a garment. They are a wonderful figment of divine power, even as were the clouds that accompanied His Transfiguration and Ascension.

d) "All the angels" (Mt 25:31) of Heaven will come with the Son of Man to judge mankind, and there are good reasons for believing that they will be visible in radiantly beautiful and glorious bodies. Their very presence and participation in the judgment will add to the visible splendor of this great and final act of God. They will form a royal retinue, a brilliant escort for the King of Kings, and by their number and incomparable beauty they will testify to His might and majesty. They will not be idle spectators but active participants in the work of the judgment: "ministering spirits" (Heb 1:14) who, as the servants of divine mercy and justice, will share in the work of Redemption from its inception to its close.

e) Finally, He will come "with much power" (Mt 24:30; *cum virtute multa*), "with great power" (Lk 21:27; *cum potestate magna*). Here, at His Second Coming, Christ will manifest His "divine power" (2 Pt 1:3), before which the mightiest forces of nature and the proudest spirits must bow low. He will appear as the great "Judge of the living and the dead," the invincible leader, triumphant over sin, death, and hell, celebrating a glorious victory over all His enemies, who are now defeated and consigned to eternal shame.

Every detail and circumstance of this final triumph will point unerringly to the unconquerable and irresistible power of Christ.

The picture of Christ as the Judge is not complete. The repetition of the soul-stirring circumstances that will immediately precede and accompany the Last Judgment is intended to evoke in the hearts of the hearers a wholesome fear and trembling. To heighten this impression, it is emphatically stated that "the Judge shall come to investigate all things rigidly."

Cuncta stricte discussurus.

The Bible describes the procedure at the Last Judgment in several passages, most elaborately in the Gospel of St. Matthew (25:31–36).

These biblical word-pictures (on which the author of the *Dies Iræ* relies) are designed to visualize as much as possible the strange and mysterious proceedings, and therefore we must not expect a literal but a figurative interpretation. The prophets often mixed symbolical and literal expressions, so that prudent scholars can arrive at their true spiritual meaning with some effort, which is useful and salutary.[21] On the one hand, we may not without necessity depart from the literal interpretation, since there is question of a material visible element, while on the other hand, we are not to forget that the Judge will be the God-Man, and therefore His actions on Judgment Day will not be merely human but theandric. Even though the Last Judgment is often described in purely human terms, we have to conceive it without the imperfections that ordinarily accompany human acts. The course of the Last Judgment will not merely be solemn, in keeping with the seriousness of the occasion and the personality of the Judge, but *extraordinary* and *wonderful.*

These remarks may be of use in the solution of the question whether and in what manner a preliminary investigation (*discussio*) will precede the sentence. Holy Scripture speaks of such an investigation, for the Day of Judgment is called "day of trial" (Ws 3:18; *ἡμέρα διαγνώσεως; dies agnitionis*).

Every human trial necessarily presupposes a judicial investigation of the facts to establish the degree of guilt. The Fathers and theologians generally call this a "trial," while the judgment itself is referred to as "the sentence." A human judge must carefully examine and weigh the evidence so that he may be able to pass a just sentence. Christ, the God-Man, does not need such an investigation; His soul clearly and truthfully sees all that happens in the whole world, for in it "are hid all the treasures of wisdom and knowledge" (Col 2:3). "Neither is there any creature invisible in His sight; but all things are naked and open to His eyes, to Whom our speech is" (Heb 4:13). In the Last Judgment, therefore, there is no need of an investigation, of witnesses, prosecution, or defense. Those expressions of Holy Writ and of the liturgy that speak of a judicial process are to be understood in a figurative sense. Particularly when used in reference to Christ, these expressions are intended to emphasize the fact that, as Judge, He knows our most secret thoughts. He is the omniscient God Who "knew all men" and "needed not that any should give testimony of man: for He knew what was in man" (Jn 2:24–25). The truth is also brought home to us that the Divine Judge, by virtue of an extraordinary interior enlightenment, will make clear to all who appear before Him at the Last Judgment—much clearer than any human investigation could—the exact measure of each one's merit or guilt and the fitting reward or punishment. Only in this sense may it be said of the Divine Judge that He will strictly (*stricte*) investigate "all things" (*cuncta*).

He will weigh all things without exception, for the Last Judgment means not merely the punishment of the guilty but the rewarding of the good. The subject matter of the judgment is man's moral conduct, his interior and exterior life and actions. "And all things that are done, God will bring into judgment for every error, whether it be good or evil" (Eccles 12:14). The most secret thoughts and desires, motives and plans, nay even omissions, will be brought to light. Not the slightest act will be overlooked or forgotten. The infallible Judge will demand an account for "every idle word" (Mt 12:36) and will reward every good deed. "Whosoever shall give ... a cup of cold water only in the name of a disciple ... shall not lose his reward" (Mt 10:42). All the circumstances that either heighten or lessen the degree of merit or guilt are duly taken into consideration: personal qualities, the manifold graces, temptations, occasions of sin, and difficulties. "For we must all be manifested before the judgment seat of Christ, that everyone may receive ... according as he hath done, whether it be good or evil" (2 Cor 5:10).

Not only does the Great Judge know all things and decide all with unerring certainty, but He will manifest His justice, which brooks no appeal, and His severity, which is no respecter of persons. Insofar as a judicial investigation is necessary for a proper knowledge of the case and a just sentence, the Judge takes extreme care and shows His love of justice. Therefore, when He is said to investigate all things rigorously (*stricte*), to examine, to weigh, to take into consideration (*discussurus*) all the circumstances of the case, the author evidently means to emphasize that God, because of His omniscience, manifests His infinite justice and inexorable rigor. These are the important phases of the Last Judgment that are developed and reiterated in the *Dies Iræ*. "I will search Jerusalem with lamps" (Soph 1:12), and "thou shalt not go out from thence till thou repay the last farthing" (Mt 5:26). What a powerful appeal these words make to us to be faithful in little things, to fulfill even the least important of our duties conscientiously, to avoid even the smallest sin. "He that feareth God, neglecteth nothing" (Eccles 7:19; *Qui timet Deum nihil negligit*). The Last Judgment cannot be avoided and will irrevocably decide an eternity of joy or pain. This doctrine might fittingly be called *the dogma of fear.* It presents for our consideration the most serious and impressive truths in the whole realm of theology. *Tremens factus sum ego et timeo, dum discussio venerit atque ventura ira*; "I am made to tremble, and I fear, till the judgment be upon us, and the coming wrath."[22] No matter from what point of view we consider the Great Judge and the Last Judgment, we are compelled to cry out with the Psalmist: "enter not into judgment with Thy servant: for in Thy sight no man living shall be justified" (Ps 142:2). Let us, therefore, "converse in fear during the time of your sojourning here" (1 Pt 1:17), so "that we may have confidence in the Day of Judgment" (1 Jn 4:17) and may not be confounded by the Master at His coming (see 1 Jn 2:28). Let us fear the all-knowing and just Judge now, so that we may be in a position to meet Him with joy and confidence when He comes to judge us!

THE THIRD STANZA

The author of the *Dies Iræ*, like the evangelist (Mt 24:30–31), does not follow a strict chronological order in the presentation of eschatological events. As foremost among them, chosen because of its significance, he emphasizes the glorious return of Christ to complete the work of the Redemption. But before He appears as Judge upon the scene, the dead must be resurrected and summoned, for it is fitting that those who are to be judged shall be assembled to meet their Judge upon His arrival. *Media autem nocte clamor factus est: ecce sponsus venit, exite obviam ei* (Mt 25:6). At midnight—that is, most unexpectedly—the summons will go forth to all who are in their graves, to rise and hasten to meet the Judge.

Tuba mirum spargens sonum
Per sepulchra regionum,
Coget omnes ante thronum.

A mighty trumpet-call will be heard everywhere, in the sepuchres of the dead and in every quarter of the world, to awaken the dead and summon them all to appear before the throne of the Judge.

This wondrous call, announcing the arrival and the omnipotent command of the Judge, will summon all men without exception, the just as well as the wicked, to appear before the judgment seat of Christ. This is evidenced by a number of biblical as well as liturgical texts. "[The Son of Man] shall send His angels with a trumpet and a great voice, and they shall gather together His elect from the four winds; from the farthest parts of the heavens to the utmost bounds of them" (Mt 24:31). This resurrection and transfiguration is to take place suddenly and unexpectedly, "in a moment, in the twinkling of an eye, at the last trumpet [the sound of the trumpet that announces the Last Judgment]: for the trumpet shall sound, and the dead shall rise again incorruptible" (1 Cor 15:52). "The Lord Himself shall come down from Heaven with commandment, and with the voice of an archangel (*in voce archangeli*) and with the trumpet of God (*in tuba Dei*), and the dead who are in Christ shall rise first" (1 Thes 4:15); that is, at the command of Christ, the archangel will loudly and compellingly raise, i.e., sound the trumpet of God, to awaken the dead and gather them all before the throne of the Judge. On this Last Day of the world, "all that are in the graves shall hear the voice of the Son of God. And they that have done good things [what the Lord hath commanded], shall come forth unto the resurrection of life [i.e., they shall arise to the true, eternal life—heavenly glory]; but they that have done evil [which the Lord hath forbidden] unto the resurrection of judgment [i.e., they shall arise to be forever reprobates—to eternal death]" (Jn 5:28–29).

The Church in her liturgy touchingly appeals to God, the Creator and Redeemer of all the faithful, to "grant to the bodies who rest in this consecrated earth and await the trumpet-call of the archangel on high (*corporibus tubam primi archangeli expectantibus*), the riches of consolation."[23] The prayer for the consecration of cemeteries is as follows: "O Lord God, shining Light of Wisdom, Guardian of Prudence, Health of the sick, Strength of the strong, Comforter of the afflicted, Life of the just, Glory of the lowly, we humbly beseech Thee to safeguard this resting-place from every stain and every snare of the unclean spirits, to purify and bless it, and to grant eternal integrity to the bodies of those who are brought to this place, so that all who are baptized and have persevered in the Catholic faith to the end of their days, and at the close of their earthly pilgrimage consigned their bodies to this holy place of rest, may at the sound of the angelic trumpets (*angelicis tubis concrepantibus*), attain the reward of the joys of Heaven. Through Christ our Lord. Amen."[24] And again the Church pleads that God "may enroll all who are buried in this cemetery in the ranks of the saints, so that on the Last Day, when the trumpets of the angels resound through the world (*cum tubæ perstrepuerint angelorum*), they may eternally praise Him, the Giver of Life."[25] In one of the Mass formularies of the Mozarabic liturgy, we find the petition that the deceased, at the time of the divine judgment, when the resounding voices of the angels shake the foundations of the earth (*quando superni examinis tempore angelicus clangor concusserit mundum*) may arise gloriously and go forward to meet the Master with the happy assurance that he will find a place at the right hand of the Judge. When the saintly Dominican nun, Margaret Fink of Töss, was asked why she tried constantly to keep awake, she answered: "Whenever I lie down, I imagine I hear the trumpets of the angels as they will sound on the Last Day, and I cannot rest, and therefore get up again."[26]

A careful comparison of these texts forces us to believe that the voice of the archangel and of the Son of God is not to be understood in a purely spiritual or figurative sense, that is to say, we cannot regard it as a mere interior act of the will or a command of Christ without any evident exterior manifestation. The texts we have quoted are designed to teach that trumpet-sounds perceptible by the senses will give the signal for the universal resurrection of the dead. We can readily picture to ourselves how, under the leadership of the archangel Michael, a host of angels will sound the trumpet-call to judgment in every quarter of the world. We naturally think of St. Michael, the prince of the angels, because there is question here of the consummation of the Church Triumphant by means of the resurrection of the dead, and St. Michael has ever been the appointed standard-bearer and protector of the Church who leads the souls of the redeemed to God. The angels appear and act merely as servants, messengers, and heralds of Christ, the "Son of God," Whose "voice," i.e., mighty command, they promulgate and make known to all. Their message is operative "through the invisible power of the majesty of God" (*invisibilis potentia magnificentiæ cælestis operatur*).[27] Immediately after the call of the angels, all the dead will rise. So mighty and so "wonderful" will the trumpets of the angels sound that they will be heard everywhere, spiritually by the souls of men, and then, when the souls have been reunited with their bodies, also materially, for the risen shall "hear" and obey the divine command to assemble at the place of judgment.

Ever since the sentence "dust thou art, and unto dust thou shalt return" was passed upon the human race (Gn 3:19), the earth has been "the land of the dying," a vast cemetery, a densely-populated city of the dead. Everywhere it is strewn with the scattered remains, the dust and ashes of the children of men. What a unique spectacle, therefore, will the earth present at the end of time, when the heavenly trumpets will resound through all the sepulchres and recall the dead to life! The call of the Son of God will awaken them all, and they will come forth from their graves from the bowels of the earth and the depths of the sea, or wherever else they may have been buried. No place will be permitted to keep its dead. Even the sea gives up the dead that are in it, and death and hell give up their dead, and they are judged, everyone according to his works (see Apoc 20:13). All will arise and be judged, for the judgment is *universal*, i.e., it extends to all men, the just and the wicked. The prophetic apostle saw "the dead" (i.e., all who had died), great and small, "standing in the presence of the throne" (Apoc 20:12). "*All* nations" will be gathered together by the angels before the throne of God (Mt 25:32). "We *must all* be manifested before the judgment-seat of Christ" (2 Cor 5:10, emphasis added).

All men who have ever lived upon the earth—even the unbaptized infants—must appear "before the throne" (*ante thronum*) of the Great Judge. The *throne* is a sign of authority. Therefore the Lord will exercise His authority as Judge over the world of angels and men, seated on a magnificent throne fashioned from the luminous clouds of Heaven. He shall "sit upon the seat of His majesty" (Mt 25:31). St. John says that this throne will be "great" and "white" (Apoc 20:11), that is to say, it will outshine in splendor and size the thrones of those who sit in judgment with Christ. The transfigured hosts of the risen will surround the throne, for "when the Lord Jesus shall be revealed from heaven, with the angels of His power," He shall come "in a flame of fire" not only "giving vengeance to them who know not God, and who obey not the gospel of our Lord Jesus Christ," but also "to be glorified in His saints, and to be made wonderful in all them who have believed" (2 Thes 1:7–8, 10).

How different will be the appearance of the just and the wicked before the Judge on that day! "Many of those that sleep in the dust of the earth shall awake: some unto life everlasting, and others unto reproach" (Dn 12:2). All will answer the trumpet-call: the just gladly and willingly, the enemies of Christ unwillingly and under compulsion (*coget*). With joy and gladness, the elect will hear the voice that announces to them the Easter morning of their glorious resurrection, whereas the wicked, in fear and confusion at the near approach of the angry Judge, will seek to escape and "say to the mountains and the rocks: Fall upon us and hide us from the face of Him that sitteth upon the throne, and from the wrath of the Lamb" (Apoc 6:16). "Behold," in order to save and glorify those whom He has redeemed, the Lord "cometh with the clouds" (on clouds of light and fire, the signs of His glory and judgment) in triumphing over His enemies, "and every eye shall see Him, and they also that pierced Him, and all the tribes of the earth shall bewail themselves because of Him" (Apoc 1:7). Seated on the throne of His majesty in the clouds, the Son of Man shall appear as Judge; "then we who are alive, who are left," i.e., the elect with transfigured bodies, "shall be taken up together with them in the clouds to meet Christ, into the air, and so shall we be always with the Lord" (1 Thes 4:16). The reprobate sinners, on the other hand, with their hideous, clumsy bodies, will remain on earth until the judgment is over (see Ws 5:1ff.).

It is dogmatically certain that our earth will be the stage for the setting of the scene on Judgment Day. It is not so certain, however, where the judgment is to be held, for revelation tells us nothing about it. "We visited the valley of Josaphat," says Jost Artus, a fifteenth century traveler, "and looking about us, began to wonder how it would be possible to assemble here all human beings who ever lived and who will live in the future, since the place seemed scarcely large enough to hold all the people of Suabia [his home country]. But after we had consulted the priests, who were conversant with Holy Writ, we were satisfied, for according to Scripture every valley shall be exalted and every mountain shall be made low, and then the valley of Josaphat will be roomy enough for all men." This pious opinion is based on Joel 3:2 and 12, in which we read: "I will gather together all nations, and will bring them down into the valley of Josaphat" and "let the nations come up into the valley of Josaphat: for there I will sit to judge all nations round about." These texts, however, offer no conclusive proof for the opinion quoted, for the word "Josaphat," i.e., Jehovah judges, does not signify a place near Jerusalem but any place where God renders judgment. Yet the interpretation in question appeals to the Christian sentiment for internal reasons; for it is assuredly a beautiful thought that our Lord should choose to finish His work of Redemption in or near the place where He suffered and died, arose from the dead, and ascended to Heaven.

The thought of the "last trumpet" that will one day summon all men to the resurrection and the judgment ought to rouse us from the fatal sleep of sin and transform our indifference and lukewarmness, our negligence and sloth into earnest watchfulness and zealous pursuit of virtue.

THE FOURTH STANZA

The fourth stanza of the *Dies Iræ* is a fitting sequel to the third, since it elucidates and enlarges upon the idea of the universal resurrection by throwing into relief its supernatural character and immediate purpose.

Mors stupebit et natura,
Cum resurget creatura
Iudicanti responsura.

Since the days of the apostles, the important and difficult dogma of "the resurrection of the body" has ever been considered one of the fundamental truths of the Christian religion. "If we wish to be Christians, we must believe that the resurrection of the dead in the flesh will take place when Christ comes to judge the living and the dead."[28] "The hope of Christians lies in the resurrection of the dead: through it [the resurrection] we are believers. The truth forces us to believe that the dead will rise again, and this truth is revealed to us by God,"[29] and it has ever been an object of firm belief, ardent hope, and joyful expectation to all good Christians: *expecto resurrectionem mortuorum*; "I expect the resurrection of the dead."[30] The deeply mysterious character of this dogma, as well as its practical application to the all-important question of reward and punishment of body and soul in the next world, have made it a stumbling-block for unbelievers and an object of persistent denial.

At the general resurrection, "Death and Nature shall stand aghast" (*mors stupebit et natura*), surprised and puzzled at this unusual and mysterious phenomenon. The amazement of death and nature is a forceful and poetic way of expressing the truth that the quickening of the dead, particularly the organic restitution of a body long since disintegrated and the reuniting of it with the soul for a life of glory, in which death shall be no more, is no natural phenomenon but a miracle of divine omnipotence. The resurrection of the reprobate sinners to everlasting bodily life is in itself a great miracle and essentially supernatural, for it can—particularly after the total disintegration and corruption of the body—be brought about only through the immediate and personal application of divine power. Still more wonderful and *absolutely supernatural* (that is to say, supernatural not merely in its manner but also in its effects) is the resurrection of the elect, for in this there is superadded a mysterious heavenly transfiguration of the body.

> Not only this is wonderful that the bodies of men decay and then rise again; that they are invested with better and more excellent qualities; and that everyone receives back his own body and not that of another; but it is still more wonderful that a transformation so grand and marvelous, one that plainly transcends all human comprehension, is accomplished 'in a moment'—i.e., in an immeasurably short time. To express this truth still more plainly, St. Paul says, 'in the twinkling of an eye,' that is, the time it takes to close the eye-lid.[31]

Death and Nature are here personified, that is, represented as persons, who are surprised and overcome by this unexpected and extraordinary spectacle of universal resurrection (*cum resurget creatura*). *Novum genus potentiæ—hactenus victoriosa mors obstupescit*; "This is power of a new kind—hitherto victorious death is astounded."[32] From the beginning until the end of time (see Rom 5:14), Death reigns victoriously over the human race, and no one escapes his power. For "who is the man that shall live and not see death?" (Ps 88:49). Death devours millions and millions of men, but on the last day he will have to give them all up again (see Apoc 20:13); all his plunder will be taken from him, and the mighty conqueror will not merely be disarmed and defeated, but totally destroyed and annihilated. Death will become powerless and vanish forever (see Is 25:8). *Mors ultra non erit* (Apoc 21:4). The damned "shall seek death and shall not find it: and they shall desire to die, and death shall fly from them" (Apoc 9:6; *et fugiet mors ab eis*). All the enemies of Christ and of His Kingdom shall be laid at the feet of the great Victor, and the last enemy to be destroyed will be Death (see 1 Cor 15:26). As soon as the universal resurrection is an accomplished fact, death will be "swallowed up in victory" (1 Cor 15:54), that is, he will cease to exist, no trace of him will remain, he has no hope of return. "Inspired by God, the apostle sees the future as fulfilled, and joyously intones a paean of victory over his fallen foe, crying aloud: 'O death, where is thy victory, O death, where is thy sting?' Gone, destroyed forever is all that thou hast done."[33]

Quite differently than Death, whose power and tyranny will be totally destroyed on Judgment Day, will Nature "stand amazed" at "the glory to come that shall be revealed in us" (Rom 8:18). All Nature, the whole created universe, will be filled with joyous astonishment, for the hour has come at last for which it has sighed and longed—the hour of its redemption from the curse of sin, from mortality and decay, from the vicissitudes of time—in a word, the hour of its renovation, transformation, transfiguration. For the end of creation is not annihilation but participation in the glory that will clothe the elect on the day of the resurrection; for then shall Nature all about us and with us shine forth with supernatural beauty and splendor (see Rom 8:19ff.) With exulting amazement all creatures will pay homage to the glory of the Redeemer, Whom they so long desired, and Who has come at last to judge the world and to place the seal of perfection upon His Kingdom. "Let the heavens rejoice, and let the earth be glad, let the sea be moved to the fullness thereof: the fields and all things that are in them shall be joyful. Then shall all the trees of the woods rejoice before the face of the Lord, because He cometh: because He cometh to judge the earth" (Ps 95:11–13).

The annihilation of death and the renewal of nature are natural consequences of the universal resurrection. The recall to life and the transfiguration of the elect is not the result of a natural development but a direct, free, and astoundingly great act of omnipotence on the part of the triune God, or of the God-Man—a mystery we must humbly believe.

The Catholic Church teaches that every soul will be reunited with essentially the same body which it inhabited on earth. That this future body cannot be substantially different from the present body is evident from the very nature and purpose of the resurrection. *Necesse est, quod idem corpus numero resurgat: alioquin non esset resurrectio vera*; "it is necessary that the same individual body be raised from the dead, or else there would be no true resurrection."[34] Only then may we speak of a *true* resurrection, when the *same* body which died and was buried in the earth is actually restored and reunited (forever) with the *same* soul with which it was united during life. *Non alia vivificatur caro, quam ipsa, quæ erat mortua*; "no other flesh is quickened than that which shall have undergone death."[35]

That "all men will rise again with their own bodies (*cum corporibus suis*)"[36] also follows from the proximate purpose of the resurrection. The self-same body which cooperated with the soul in good and evil actions is to be rewarded or punished in the life to come. Before the judgment-seat of Christ, every man will receive "the proper things of the body," that is to say, reward or punishment "according as he hath done, whether it be good or evil" (2 Cor 5:10). It follows that the body must share in the reward and punishment, in the joys and sufferings of the soul in the life beyond. The body that has been mortified and crucified by penance in this life, will be resplendent with glory in the next—*exsultabunt Domino ossa humiliate*;[37] the body, on the other hand, that was given over to the sinful gratification of lust will suffer eternal punishment.

The just and the wicked will rise *simultaneously,* i.e., at the same moment, but what a mighty difference in their resurrection, particularly in the appearance of the body! The damned have sown "in his flesh," and "of the flesh also shall they reap corruption" (Gal 6:8). They will arise to a life which is called "second death" (Apoc 20:14; *mors secunda*), because in spite of their bodily immortality and incorruptibility, they actually suffer eternal death and constant decay. "For the Lord Almighty ... will give fire, and worms into their flesh, that they may burn and may feel forever" (Jdt 16:20–21). Their life is worse than death, for they live forever only to suffer. The bodies of the damned are hideous, disgusting, unwieldy, for they are condemned to receive the full measure of punishment, disgrace as well as suffering. This hideous body, teeming with corruption, shall give testimony of the hideous soul it harbors before Heaven and earth.

Totally different in appearance will be the elect, who will arise with glorified bodies to enjoy an eternity of happiness. They will resemble the risen Savior, Who is their prototype and model: for Christ "will reform the body of our lowness made like to the body of His glory" (Phil 3:21). First of all, they will arise without any corporal defects and weaknesses, having perfect use of every organ, member, and sense, in natural perfection, youth, and beauty. To these characteristics are added the supernatural gifts of the elect. We have not now a full knowledge of the glory of the risen body, but we ought not for that reason to remain silent, says St. Augustine, when there is question of praising God in the joyous hope of the resurrection: *spei nostræ gaudium propter Dei laudem non est tacendum;* "our hope should utter itself to the praise of God, and not be silent."[38] Therefore, we may point out at least the transcendent endowments or qualities of the risen bodies of the elect, following St. Paul in his First Epistle to the Corinthians:

"Sown [buried] in corruption, it [the body] shall rise in *incorruption*" (1 Cor 15:42, emphasis added).

This privilege of the glorified body means something more than the immortality it enjoyed in paradise; for in consequence of this fixed and inherent incorruption, the glorified body is now placed beyond the reach not only of death and corruption but of suffering, discomfort, pain, and sickness of every sort. This quality of everlasting *impassibility*, or incapacity for suffering, is a supernatural gift that makes our body a worthy dwelling-place for the glorified soul.

"Sown in dishonor, it shall rise in *glory*" (1 Cor 15:43, emphasis added). By "glory," we are to understand not the sum-total of all the supernatural gifts of God to the risen bodies of the saints, but a special gift or quality called *brightness* (*claritas*) that clothes them with a splendor and beauty visible to the corporal eye. To give us at least a faint idea of this wonderful gift, Holy Scripture compares it to the highest earthly beauty, viz., the radiant splendor of the stars in the firmament of Heaven. Christ on Mount Tabor (see Mt 17:2) foreshadowed this prerogative, and we are told the just "shall shine" (Ws 3:7; *fulgebunt*) "as the sun" (Mt 13:43) and "as the brightness of the firmament ... as stars for all eternity" (Dn 12:3). This supermundane radiance proceeding from the soul supremely happy at the Beatific Vision of God overflows into the body, rendering its outward form and appearance transcendently beautiful.

"Sown in weakness, it shall rise in *power*" (1 Cor 15:43, emphasis added). By this quality of the glorified body, we usually understand a wonderful strength and agility, by which the body, freed from its innate clumsiness and from the fetters imposed by the law of gravitation, moves with imperceptible quickness and utmost facility in whatever direction it is drawn by the soul. The glorified body is the immediate work of God's omnipotence, "a building of God, a house not made with hands, eternal in heaven"

(2 Cor 5:1), which, unlike our present corruptible habitation, is no longer "a load upon the soul" nor "presseth down the mind that museth upon many things" (Ws 9:15).

"It is sown a natural body, it shall rise a *spiritual* body" (1 Cor 15:44, emphasis added). The term "spiritual" is sometimes used in the sense of "glorified," but here we are to understand it in a more restricted sense; namely, as denoting a perfection that gives the glorified body a supernatural delicacy, refinement, or transparency (*subtilitas*), by which it is able to overcome all corporeal hindrances to its movements in space, penetrating material objects at will and capable of mutual penetration. The risen body actually becomes like the spirit—spiritualized by a supernatural participation in the higher life of the soul, without, however, being transformed into spirit, for it is and remains a *true* body, which by nature is tangible, solid, and extended in space.

This perishable body, therefore, having thus become not only immortal but incapable of suffering, resplendent with beauty and power, bright as the sun, and no longer subject to the limitations of space, will arise from the dust and corruption of the grave to blossom forever in fullness of life and perfect beauty. These gifts and prerogatives of the glorified body, which are sometimes granted to the saints in life, though only in an imperfect manner and usually but for a very short time, will in the next life be the inheritance of the elect—an inheritance to be enjoyed forever, a happy reward for the hardships, sufferings, sacrifices, and mortifications of this earthly life. They are in a sense the dowry of the body, enabling it to enjoy to the fullest extent the delights of the soul at the heavenly marriage feast.

> Even now the eyes of faith see the first faint dawn of a magnificent Easter morning which brightens the abode of the weary pilgrim on earth; the ear of faith seems to catch the

> songs of the angels and to hear the mighty voice of the Judge summoning all who sleep in death to arise to a new and brighter life. The soul awaits its former companion, the body, that it may infuse fresh life into it, and take it along to the heavenly Paradise, there to dwell in inseparable union with it and to be forever happy in God's presence, in the company of all the angels and saints. Just as the true liberty and joy of the spirit consist in the service of God, so the liberty and joy of the body consist in the service of the spirit; as the soul grows more like God, the body grows more like the soul."[39]

Men will arise to give an account of their stewardship to the Great Judge. The expression employed here, "to answer to the Judge" (*respondere*), recalls those passages of Holy Writ where the judgment is described in the form of a dialogue adapted to our understanding (see Mt 25:31–46). The general resurrection is the first act of the general judgment. The whole man, i.e., man as composed of body and soul, must appear before the judgment-seat of Jesus Christ at the end of the world; for before the body can enter into the realm of everlasting glory or the eternal fire of hell, judgment must be passed upon it, even as judgment was passed upon the soul immediately after death. And since the Judge Himself will appear visibly upon earth, so those who are to be judged will also appear in visible, bodily shape, so that in this respect, too, the Last Judgment is truly a public judgment. It will be a rigorous and severe judgment, for the Judge is omniscient, almighty, all-holy, and all-just. When St. Paul, standing before the heathen governor Felix, spoke of "the resurrection of the just and unjust," and of "the judgment to come," Felix was terrified (Acts 24:15, 25). It will not be an easy matter to give an account of oneself at this judgment, for even the just man, if he would attempt to answer the thousandfold accusations of the heavenly Judge, would find it impossible to justify himself. *Si [homo] voluerit contendere cum eo, non poterit ei respondere unum pro mille* (Jb 9:3).

The doctrine of the resurrection and that of the Last Judgment are extremely important truths of divine revelation, the serious consideration of which is bound to make a lasting impression upon the thoughts and actions of men, inciting them to do good and to avoid evil. But while the doctrine of the resurrection is primarily a dogma of *hope,* that of the Last Judgment appears as a dogma of *fear.* This distinction coincides with the terminology of the Bible, which employs *resurrection* in a good and *judgment* predominantly in an evil sense, i.e., as damnation. The joyful and confident expectation of the coming glory of the resurrection strengthens, encourages, and comforts the weary pilgrim on earth in the manifold miseries of life as well as in the sorrows and terrors of death, while the devout expectation of the resurrection is woven into the very texture of the Church's liturgy for the burial of the dead, from the blessing of the corpse at the portals of the church to the blessing of the grave that is to be its final resting-place; the dawn of that glorious Easter morn even now sheds its effulgent rays of glory upon the darkness of the grave. The *hope of the resurrection* that hovers over the grave like a golden cloud lends an unearthly loveliness and dignity to death; it mitigates the grief we experience at the passing of our loved ones (see 1 Thes 4:12ff.); it prompts us to treat their earthly remains reverently and affectionately and to carry our own bodies clean and unsullied before the judgment-seat of God.

THE FIFTH STANZA

The description of the general judgment that was begun in the second stanza and then interrupted is now continued and brought to a close:

Liber scriptus proferetur,
In quo totum continetur,
Unde mundus iudicetur.

"A written book shall be brought forth, wherein is contained the information, in the light of which the world will be judged."

Holy Scripture repeatedly describes the procedure and circumstances of the Last Judgment, sometimes employing rich metaphors drawn from the resemblance between divine and human judgments. For this reason, many of the expressions used are not to be taken literally but in a figurative sense. This caution refers principally to the *book* or *books* mentioned in the description of the Last Judgment. "If we were to accept this term in a literal sense (*carnaliter*), who could measure the volume or its contents? Or how long a time would be required to read a book in which there are recorded in detail the transactions of every man's life?"[40] The prophetic writers of the Old Testament speak of the opening of books at judgment. "The judgment sat, and the books were opened" (Dn 7:10). St. John saw "the dead, great and small, standing in the presence of the throne, and the books were opened; and another book was opened, which is the book of life (*et alius liber apertus est, qui est vitæ*); and the dead were judged by those things which were written in the books," and they received their eternal reward or punishment "according to their works" (Apoc 20:12).

The metaphor of the book of judgment in the *Dies Iræ* is undoubtedly taken from these biblical texts and must therefore be interpreted accordingly. According to the interpretation of the truth underlying the respective references of Holy Scripture, we speak either of one or of several books. The book that is opened for the judgment is one—namely, God's omniscience—and at the same time many—namely, the individual consciences of men. The mention of a volume in which are written all things that are necessary for the knowledge and consideration of the court effectively, though figuratively, expresses the truth that the Divine Judge not merely *knows* the merits and demerits of every rational creature but that He will manifest them to all the world so clearly and perfectly that, after the passing of the sentence, both the elect and the damned will be forced to confess: "Thou art just, O Lord, and Thy judgment is right" (Ps 118:137). The content of this stanza emphasizes and sheds further light on the truth, previously proposed, that the "Judge of the world" will investigate all things rigidly (*cuncta stricte discussurus*), i.e., that He is omniscient and all-holy.

"The eyes of the Lord are far brighter than the sun" (Ecclus 23:28); His all-piercing eye penetrates even the innermost recesses of the soul and gazes unceasingly upon all that moves upon the stream of time. On the Day of Judgment, by an extraordinary grace, He will permit the men and angels who are gathered about His throne to participate to a certain extent in "the riches of the wisdom and knowledge of God" (Rom 11:33). By a divine illumination, every man will know first of all the things that concern himself, his past, and the present condition of his soul; as in an *open book*, he will be able to read the record of his own conscience, the history of his interior and exterior life, all his thoughts, words, and actions, his merits and demerits, the measure of the reward due him for his virtues and of the punishment incurred by his sins, and thus he will be enabled to understand fully the justice of the judgment passed upon him. He will likewise be enlightened concerning the condition and circumstances of his fellow men—nay, even of the angels of God—for he will be able to read the record of good and evil that is written in the exposed conscience of every individual who appears before the judgment-seat of God. Thus, the record of every conscience will be exposed like an *open book* to the view of angels and of men. "We must assume a certain divine power, by which the individual is enabled to recall to mind all his works, both good and evil, and see them all as it were in one swift glance, and that consequently the conscience of every man will accuse or excuse him, and thus every man individually, and all men together, will be judged. This divine power is called a *book*, for in it every man reads whatever his conscience by means of this power recalls."[41]

Besides the range of material *objects* that are taken into consideration at the Last Judgment, this stanza of the *Dies Iræ* indicates all the personal *subjects* who are judged, in the words: "the world (*mundus*) will be judged." When the curtain falls upon the last act of that great historical drama of world history, which has lasted for several thousand years, it will mark the end of the universe and of every creature, that is to say, every creature will enter upon its final destiny assigned to it by the Creator, the Redeemer, and the Judge. The reference here made is not to the world in the restricted sense, i.e., to the world of nature, the visible corporal things of the universe that have their place in the final judgment inasmuch as they shall be purified and renewed by fire; but when speaking of the Last Judgment as a judgment of the world, it is understood to refer primarily to all rational creatures, including the angels.

Just as all men will die and rise again, so all men will be summoned to appear before the Great Judge, where, in consequence of a supernatural illumination of the mind, his true status will be made manifest, and reward or punishment will be meted out to him according to his desert. Because of the omniscience of the Divine Judge no formal examination will take place at the Last Judgment; we speak of such an examination only in a figurative or applied sense, as the all-knowing Judge brings to light all things, both good and evil. It is quite evident that Holy Scripture, in referring to or describing the details of the Last Judgment, has in mind chiefly adults. This explains the frequent and emphatic references to a "judgment of God, Who will render to every man according to his works" (Rom 2:5–6; see Apoc 22:12); in the strictest sense, only those are to be judged who "have done good or evil" and therefore "must render an account of *their own works* (*de factis propriis*)."[42] Only inasmuch as "every reward presupposes a judicial act" can we speak (in a restricted sense) of infants and those not responsible for their acts as being judged, not because they were personally free to act but because they did or did not possess sanctifying grace. For it is from this point of view that their eternal destiny will be decided and publicly manifested on Judgment Day; they will either be taken into or excluded from Heaven.

It is an accepted truth that, besides the human race, the angels, too, will appear at the Last Judgment, and in a certain sense be judged, though there is a difference of opinion regarding the matter and form of the judgment to be passed upon them. Some theologians hold that judgment will be passed upon the pure spirits in the same manner as upon men, whereas others exclude any actual reward or punishment from the judgment passed upon them, holding that the angels receive merely an accidental increase of reward or punishment, inasmuch as they participate only indirectly in the judgment passed upon men. There are perhaps more convincing reasons for the opinion that the angels, like men, will receive their full share of reward or punishment on Judgment Day. Hence, the Day of Judgment is a day of reckoning for the world of pure spirits as well as for mankind. The good angels have exercised a benign, the bad angels a malicious influence upon the destiny and history of man, and consequently, the former will receive an increase of honor and joy while the latter will be condemned to greater shame and suffering. Satan and his cohorts will also lose the power to dwell on the earth and in "high places" (see Eph 6:12) for the purpose of tempting men and leading them to destruction. "For ... God spared not the angels that sinned, but delivered them, drawn down by infernal ropes to the lower hell, unto torments, to be reserved unto judgment" (2 Pt 2:4), "unto the judgment of the great day" (Jude 1:6). And St. Paul says that "we shall judge [the wicked] angels" (1 Cor 6:3).

All our works, words, thoughts, desires, and even motives are entered in the book of judgment by the Divine Judge, Who "searcheth the reins and hearts" of men (Apoc 2:23), and upon this record our eternal salvation or damnation depends. In all our thoughts and actions, may we ever be guided by the thought of this heavenly diary, so that our days may be "full days" (Ps 72:10), and our works "full before God" (see Apoc 3:2); then our names will be "written in heaven" (Lk 10:20) and will not be blotted "out of the book of life" (Apoc 3:5). Let us, therefore, pray without ceasing that our names may be inscribed indelibly upon the roll of God's predestined saints.

THE SIXTH STANZA

The Last Judgment is to be a glorious vindication and glorification of divine providence; it is to be all-embracing in the disposition of good and evil, to fix the final equation of all things on earth. For this reason, the two outstanding characteristics of the Last Judgment, viz., the universal publicity given to the sentence and the inexorable strictness of the all-knowing and all-just Judge, are here again introduced and emphasized. The transition "when therefore" (*ergo cum*) indicates that this stanza will again make mention of a thought previously expressed in order to amplify and clarify its meaning.

Iudex ergo cum sedebit
Quidquid latet, apparebit:
Nil inultum remanebit.

"When, therefore, the Judge shall sit upon the judgment-seat, whatsoever is hidden shall be revealed, and no wrong shall remain unpunished." At the end of time, the Lord will come with great power, clothed with glory and majesty, seated on a luminous cloud that is His throne and the seat of judgment. He is referred to as "sitting" in judgment to indicate the nature of His office. The Judge is described as "seated" in order to indicate His judicial authority and power, His majesty and dignity, and, above all, the dispassionate, dignified, divine calmness of the highest, holiest, mightiest of judges.

Holy Scripture repeatedly makes mention of human aids and associate judges of Christ at the Last Judgment. Our Lord promised the apostles, who had left all things to follow Him, a share in His royal glory, telling them: "In the regeneration ... you also shall sit on twelve seats, judging the twelve tribes of Israel" (Mt 19:28). It is clear that He meant to promise them a special reward and distinction. While we must, of course, hold that the cooperation of the apostles in the judgment will be subordinate to the judicial activity of Christ, we are unable to tell just what their role will be. The Fathers of the Church and theologians generally hold that this special participation in the Last Judgment is to be the reward of those saints who, because of their heroic practice of poverty and humility, their complete detachment from worldly things, and their zeal in the imitation of Christ, may justly be called apostles of the Lord. Perhaps the promise of Christ can be best interpreted by assuming that the apostles and apostle-like saints will occupy a special place of honor and distinction at the Last Judgment, that is, will form a sort of jury or body of associate judges and, as such, participate in the passing and promulgation of the sentence. Voluntary poverty and perfect detachment from the world in order to follow Christ must, therefore, be something great and glorious to merit such a great distinction and reward; for the truly apostolic poor will be specially invited to the throne of the "King of Kings," and to participate in judging the world. It goes without saying that the Blessed Virgin Mary, Mother of God, will occupy the first place among the saints; her place of honor (as usually depicted) is beside the Judge; she is the most distinguished participant in this unique triumph of her Son.

When the Eternal Judge, surrounded by the heavenly hosts, sits in judgment with such power and glory, the wicked will be seized with shame and despair, as "the hidden things of darkness" are brought "to light" (1 Cor 4:5). The words *Quidquid latet, apparebit* are evidently intended to be quite general, and must be understood in this sense. The context, however, (*nil inultum remanebit*) indicates that reference is made particularly to a manifestation of conscience, a revelation of the secrets of the heart, particularly of the wicked. For special emphasis is laid upon the sins, mistakes, and misdeeds which men usually attempt to hide from the knowledge of their fellowmen; these are called *occulta*, *abscondita*, *abdita*, *obscura*, *opera tenebrarum*, especially when they are mentioned among the things that will be brought to light on the Last Day. "For everyone that doth evil hateth the light and cometh not to the light, that his works may not be reproved" (Jn 3:20).

The Lord knoweth these "hidden things" (Dn 13:42; *absconditorum es cognitor*) and "the secrets of the heart" (Ps 43:22; *novit abscondita cordis*); therefore He can and will "bring to light the hidden things of darkness, and will make manifest the counsels of the hearts" (1 Cor 4:5). For "nothing is covered that shall not be revealed: nor hid, that shall not be known," (Mt 10:26); that is, even the most secret and hidden things will become manifest and known to all on "the day when God shall judge the secrets of men" (Rom 2:16). Here in this world, darkness often surrounds the human heart and hides it from the eyes of the world: but *there* the most secret thoughts and emotions, the most hidden folds and corners, the undiscovered motives and desires of the soul will be laid bare to the gaze of all, for falsehood and deceit, hypocrisy and dissimulation will then be impossible. Every veil will be torn away and every cover thrown back, even the whitewashed walls of the tomb will be pierced to expose to view the rottenness and corruption of the grave. The eye of the Judge sees all things, and He will summon all men before His judgment-seat. "Such is the knowledge and such the terrifying glance of the Most High Judge," says St. Leo the Great, "that it penetrates solids and pierces the things that are hidden. What is dark becomes light to Him (*obscura clarent*), what is dumb answers Him, what is silent gives testimony before Him. Let no one, therefore, rest content in the assurance that his conscience is now hidden from men: nothing will escape the eye of the all-seeing Judge."[43]

All sins will be made known on Judgment Day, even the repented, forgiven, and atoned sins and imperfections of the elect. However, the disclosure of repented sins will neither humiliate nor distress the blessed but rather, because of their love of truth and humility, give them an occasion to rejoice in God's infinite mercy and grace, which so freely and without any merit of their own assisted them in doing penance and persevering in goodness and is now made manifest and glorified before the whole world.

"There is not any thing secret that shall not be made manifest, nor hidden that shall not be known and come abroad" (Lk 8:17). These words of the Divine Master apply not only to the things that are wicked and sinful but also to those that are good and noble. The Christian's life of grace, prayer, and sacrifice, that is "hid with Christ in God" (Col 3:3), "the hidden man of the heart in the incorruptibility of a quiet and a meek spirit" (1 Pt 3:4), will shine in glory before the gaze of the world on the Day of Judgment. The most beautiful and fragrant flowers in the garden of a truly Christian soul, the greatest and most remarkable sacrifices and self-denials, the most glorious struggle for virtue and the most meritorious acts of a virtuous life are not infrequently hidden from the eyes of men, but when the Lord of Heaven and earth comes, all these will be as an open book.

The complete disclosure of all good and evil deeds, of the merit and guilt not only of the individual but of the whole human race, will first of all establish before men the justice of God in His judgments of the elect and the wicked; at the same time, it will throw into clearest relief the wise, loving, tender, and powerful yet simple workings of *Divine Providence.* All the riddles of life, now apparently so insoluble to the short-sighted understanding of mortal man, will be solved at the general judgment, for assembled humanity will there witness the placing of the seal of approval upon all previous judgments of God, which here and now will be declared perfect, final, and just. "Then too it will be made clear by what just judgment it happens that so many, yes, nearly all of the just judgments of God are hidden from the understanding of men, though pious Christians are not unaware that the hidden things of God are just."[44] In the course of history, "God's judgments, though hidden, are just, and though just, hidden"; but at the end of time will come "the last and public judgment through Jesus Christ Who will judge justly, even though He has been judged unjustly by men."[45]

Our Sequence in its description of the Last Judgment stresses its serious and terrifying aspect, as shown especially by the inexorable strictness and justice of God in punishing the wicked; for this reason, it emphasizes only one aspect of the process of perfect retribution, namely, that "nothing shall remain unpunished."

Nil inultum remanebit.

God rewards goodness and avenges evil. Every offense against His Divine Majesty must be atoned for. His supreme authority as Judge of all creation is clearly shown in the punishment of evil. The penalties which He imposes for sin are usually designated in Holy Scripture as just measures of retribution. They are meet and just, and it is a holy revenge which God, for the sake of His honor and glory, must take for every offense committed against Him. "Revenge not yourselves, my dearly beloved; but give place unto wrath, for it is written: Revenge is mine, I will repay, saith the Lord" (Rom 12:19; see Dt 32:35). God has, therefore, in every instance reserved unto Himself the right to punish evil and the evildoer, and especially to administer perfect justice in the form of a decision that comes from a supreme court and admits of no appeal. He will appear publicly and visibly on the Day of Judgment as the God of "recompenses" and will hold undisputed sway as "avenger" on "the day of vengeance of the Lord" (Is 34:8; and 1 Thes 4:6), when His avenging justice will extend itself to all things, including the smallest and most insignificant.

However, since the Lord is inclined to reward rather than to punish, He will certainly not overlook or leave unrewarded any good deed on that day when perfect retribution begins for all eternity. He punishes sin, which is our own work, comparatively less than He rewards virtue, which is His work; for He punishes the former with less severity than it demands, while He rewards the latter above that which is its due, so that the good works of the just actually receive a greater reward than they deserve. Here, too, the Eternal Judge neither overlooks nor forgets anything, though it be ever so small or unknown to men. At His coming, all the meritorious prayers, good works, sufferings and conflicts of the just will be disclosed and rewarded beyond all measure, "unto praise and glory and honor" (1 Pt 1:7); for the Divine Judge, by His final decision, will bestow upon them the acknowledgment of their virtue and crown them with heavenly glory, and thus honor them before the whole world. Such a glorious, eternal reward, however, will be given only for works performed with a pure and holy intention, before the "Father Who seeth in secret" (Mt 6:4). Those who perform works of Christian charity, piety, and self-denial "in the streets, that they may be honored by men" (Mt 6:2) need hope for no further reward, for in seeking the empty praise of men, "they have (already) received their reward" (Mt 6:2).

With the greatest exactitude, all things will be dragged into the light and weighed in "the golden balance of Heaven." The all-knowing God will examine, the all-just God will decide, the almighty God will reward and punish. "The eyes of the Lord are far brighter than the sun, beholding round about all the ways of men, and the bottom of the deep, and looking into the hearts of men, into the most hidden parts" (Ecclus 23:28). "No thought escapeth Him and no word can hide itself from Him" (Ecclus 42:20). His eyes "are open upon all the ways of the children of Adam, to render unto every one according to his ways, and according to the fruit of his devices" (Jer 32:19).

He who often and earnestly recalls these truths will endeavor to guard his soul (Dt 4:15), and even though no human eye sees him, he will carefully avoid even the smallest imperfection and conscientiously fulfill even the least of his obligations.

THE SEVENTH STANZA

Here ends the brief but impressive description of the end of the world, the general resurrection, and the Last Judgment. Meditating upon these wonderful and terrifying details, the soul involuntarily experiences fear and hope, desire and anxiety, and, quite naturally, tries to give vent to these emotions. The present stanza is the connecting link between the first and the second part of the *Dies Iræ*, between the epic and at the same time lyrical description of the Day of Judgment and the deeply-felt and effective plea for pardon which constitutes the second part of the Sequence.

Quid sum miser tunc dicturus,
Quem patronum rogaturus,
Cum vix iustus sit securus?

From this stanza to the close there is ever before the soul "the picture of the judgment (*divinæ districtionis imago*)."[46] The prayerful Christian is transported and finds himself present in spirit before the judgment-seat of God at the precise moment (*tunc*) when he is asked to render an account of his life. Standing before the strict and inexorable Judge, he realizes more fully than ever his misery, helplessness, and guilt, and it is precisely this painful recognition that prompts him to make a humble confession. Unworthy though he be, he still hopes for grace and pardon, even if his prayer is made in fear and trembling.

Quid sum miser tunc dicturus?

"What shall I, a poor sinner, say on the day when God calls me to render an account of myself?" Then the time of grace that was given me to prepare for eternity will be at an end, the time for work and merit will be forever past, and the day of wrath and of reckoning will have arrived. *Homo ... brevi vivens tempore repletur multis miseriis* (Jb 14:1). Though man's life upon earth is short, it is filled with misery. His soul is oppressed with the weight of sin and the dread of punishment. We are all laden with a dreadful burden, pressed down with the load of a corruptible body (see Ws 9:15), condemned to the labors and anxieties of life and, lastly, to the anguish of death, and after death comes the judgment. Before the judgment-seat of God, poor, sinful man at last realizes the full burden of his misery, his helplessness, and the hopelessness of a situation he must face alone; there remain for him neither grace, nor pardon, nor suspension of judgment, nor time for repentance, nor flight, nor excuse, nor defense. The vision of the luminous Cross, of the glorified wounds of the Redeemer-Judge, and the presence of the Mother of mercies and of the hosts of the elect—all these will silence forever the trembling words of defense on the lips of the sinner; he sees with overwhelming clearness the enormity of his sins and his ingratitude to the overflowing grace, which he has despised and abused. Hopelessly he realizes and confesses his guilt, his great guilt, his unpardonable guilt. "What shall I do when God shall rise to judge? and when He shall examine, what shall I answer Him?" (Jb 31:14). Therefore, "in all things look to thy end, and how thou shalt be able to stand before a severe Judge, from Whom nothing is hidden; Who takes no bribes, nor receives excuses, but will judge that which is just."[47]

Quem patronum rogaturus?

In vain will he seek or plead for an "advocate" to defend him on that day. The protection and intercession of the Mother of God and of the angels and saints is available only during our earthly pilgrimage, the time of probation, the battle of life, but no longer when we have reached our destiny, for there "divine justice" alone reigns, i.e., decides our fate for all eternity. That is why we pray *now*: "Ye holy guardian angels, protect us in the battle, that we may not be lost at the dreadful judgment."[48] "Why dost thou not provide for thyself against the Day of Judgment, when no man can be excused or defended by another, but everyone shall have enough to do to answer for himself? At present, thy labor is profitable; thy tears are acceptable; thy sighs will be heard, and thy sorrow is satisfactory, and may purge away thy sins (*nunc labor tuus fructuosus, fletus acceptabilis, gemitus exaudibilis, dolor satisfactorius et purgativus*)."[49]

We may not underestimate or consider unnecessary the help and intercession of the saints; on the contrary, the consciousness of our own impotency and weakness, our sinfulness and unworthiness, should urge us to call humbly upon the friends of God, who are our mighty patrons, helpers, and protectors in all the perils of life. God has appointed them as our intercessors and willingly hears their prayers for us *now,* if we but do our part. "It is an excellent thing," says St. John Chrysostom, "to be advantaged by the intercession of the saints, but only if we are not found wanting on our part. If we fail to do our share, their intercession cannot help us. Intercession implies help and assistance, the very notion of which presupposes that the one who is helped and assisted does not remain inactive but contributes his share, for the help that is given remains ineffective unless helper and helped cooperate. We should not, therefore, on the one hand, underestimate the intercession of the saints, nor, on the other hand, place all of our hopes upon them: this latter method would naturally cause us to grow careless and indifferent, while the former would rob us of a great spiritual gain. Let us, therefore, call upon the saints of God *now* (as long as the time of grace lasts), so that they may intercede for us and assist us, but at the same time let us be diligent in the practice of virtue, so that we may be partakers in those heavenly gifts which God has promised to those who love Him."

Great, indeed, must be the mental anguish and the helplessness of the poor, unfortunate sinner at the near approach of Judgment Day, "when even the just shall hardly be safe."

Cum vix iustus sit securus.

"What will be the misery of those who have wasted the long years, when the walls behind which they have entrenched themselves suddenly crash to earth and they face a judgment without mercy, a judgment in which even the just man shall scarcely be saved?"[50]

For a correct and full understanding of this verse, it will be helpful to go to the source from which not only this line but practically the entire stanza has been substantially taken. In his First Epistle, St. Peter says: "For the time is, that judgment should begin at the house of God [i.e., the Church]; and if first at us, what shall be the end of them that believe not the gospel of God? And if the just man (*iustus*) shall scarcely (*vix*) be saved (*salvabitur*), where shall the ungodly and sinner appear?" (1 Pt 4:17–18). In the visitations, sufferings, and persecutions which so frequently break over the faithful children of the Church, St. Peter sees the beginnings of the general judgment, which is related to the individual and successive judgments of history like the full breaking of the storm to the lightning that precedes it. From the severity with which God in His holiness and justice punishes the sins and failings and imperfections of the faithful in this world, the apostle seeks to show how terrible will be the final judgment of the wicked and unbelievers. In the catastrophe of the Last Day, that is, at the Last Judgment, these will not appear, i.e., they will not be able to answer the Great Judge, but they will be miserably destroyed. "The wicked shall not rise again in judgment: nor sinners in the council of the just" (Ps 1:5).

If the faithful servants of God will be saved in the "burning heat" (1 Pt 4:12) of trial and suffering only with much tribulation and difficulty, what will be the fate of the wicked, when God in His justice will punish their wickedness with eternal perdition! These are the thoughts that are suggested by our Sequence, though under a different form and from another point of view. The difficulty of saving our soul and attaining unto eternal bliss is impressively brought home to us. The path that leads to Heaven is straight and narrow (see Mt 7:14), and narrow also is the gate (see Lk 13:24) through which we have to enter. It requires a zealous effort, incessant pains, and a persevering struggle to enter into this "narrow gate"; for only the straight and narrow path of self-denial and labor, of humility and mortification leads to "the everlasting kingdom of our Lord and Savior Jesus Christ" (2 Pt 1:11). "The difficulty of saving our soul and the ease with which we may lose it, becomes plain when we consider the decay of human nature, the darkening of the intellect, the weakening of the will, the evil inclinations of the heart, the enticing allurements of the world, and the wily attacks of the adversary."[51]

Under such conditions, life is and will remain to the end a warfare and a trial (see Jb 7:1), and it is easy to understand that even the "just" man, i.e., the believing Christian who is in the state of sanctifying grace, is "hardly certain" of salvation during this mortal life, nay even at the time of his first appearance before the Judge. "Certainty" or assurance may be understood either objectively or subjectively. Objective certainty of salvation excludes all *danger* of losing our soul, while subjective certainty excludes merely the *fear* of losing it. Perfect freedom from every danger and from the possibility of losing our soul comes only at the moment of death, or, more correctly, when the particular judgment of God is announced, and consequently (apart from a special divine revelation), man cannot be fully and infallibly certain of his eternal salvation until then. As long as he is in this world, he is in danger of neglecting the practice of Christian virtue and thereby falling into mortal sin and incurring eternal damnation. Therefore, St. Peter admonishes Christians "to labor the more, that by good works you may make sure your calling and election" (state of grace), at the same time assuring them, that if they will be faithful in following this admonition, they will "not sin at any time," that is, not sin grievously and suffer the loss of their souls (2 Pt 1:10).

Our good works protect us against the loss of eternal salvation, which begins with the possession of grace in this world and ends with the Beatific Vision in the next. Inasmuch as these works are signs of predestination, they give the just man not indeed an unquestioned certainty but a more or less generous assurance, confidence, and contentment regarding his final perseverance and eternal happiness. St. Paul corroborates this both by word and example. "For I am not conscious to myself of anything [i.e., a grievous sin], yet am I not hereby justified; but he that judgeth me is the Lord" (1 Cor 4:4), Whose all-seeing eye penetrates to the deepest recesses of the heart and often discovers there sins of which we ourselves are not conscious. And the same apostle who was a vessel of election (Acts 9:15; *vas electionis*) and a perfect spiritual director, says: "I chastise my body, and bring it into subjection: lest perhaps, when I have preached to others, I myself should become a castaway" (1 Cor 9:27). It is thus that the Apostle of the Gentiles, who had been caught up to the third heaven (see 2 Cor 12:4), speaks and acts! The just man must, therefore, strive by zeal and perseverance in the practice of virtue, and by a living faith, to work out and assure his salvation. If he does this, he will gain the comforting and peaceful assurance that he will be able to face the Last Judgment without fear. Perfect security, excluding all doubt and fear, will be his portion after the particular judgment which takes place at the moment of death. It is then that he will hear from the lips of the Divine Judge the assurance of his final beatitude. With this assurance, nay, in the actual and unalterable possession of eternal happiness, he appears at the general judgment, if the latter occurs later in point of time than the former.

Such a blessed certainty on the Day of Judgment will be enjoyed only by those who, during their earthly life, work out their salvation "with fear and trembling" (Phil 2:12) and who "serve, pleasing God, with fear and reverence, for our God is a consuming fire," i.e., a terrible Judge Who punishes evil (Heb 12:28, 29). "Thou must preserve a good and firm hope of winning the crown; but must not think thyself secure, lest thou grow negligent or proud."[52] Blessed is the man who always fears to offend God and, with a tender conscience, avoids sin. "Serve ye the Lord with fear: and rejoice unto Him with trembling" (Ps 2:11). "According to the words of the apostle: 'He that thinketh himself to stand, let him take heed lest he fall' (1 Cor 10:12), there is no one so firmly safeguarded that he can be certain of his constancy and perseverance (*nemo est tanta firmitate suffultus ut de stabilitate sua debeat esse securus*)."[53] A well-ordered, child-like, holy fear of God safeguards and secures our salvation against the innumerable dangers and enemies that constantly surround and oppress us during life, and in the end it will enable us to take our stand with joyful confidence before the judgment-seat of Christ. That earnest and well-considered little word "then" (*tunc*) contains a powerful incentive to make diligent and zealous use of the present time of grace and trial. "Be careful now and sorry for thy sins, that on the Day of Judgment thou mayest be secure with the blessed (*ut in die iudicii securus sis cum beatis*)."[54]

THE EIGHTH STANZA

The prophets as a rule follow up their terror-inspiring descriptions of the Last Judgment with a stirring appeal for sincere repentance and conversion, which is the necessary, in fact, the only means by which the sinner can escape damnation and be saved. A similar order is followed in the *Dies Iræ*, for after the summary but effective presentation of the "last things," there follows a tender and touching petition for mercy and pardon for "the afflicted spirit," for the "contrite and humbled heart" (Ps 50:19), in order that they may not be lost on "the great and dreadful day of the Lord" (Jl 2:31).

God's judgments are like the mountains and "the great deep" (Ps 35:7)—unfathomable, incomprehensible, unsearchable (see Rom 11:33), particularly in the severity of the final sentence on all human acts. Therefore, the very thought of the approach of the Divine Judge and His judgment strikes terror into the soul of mortal man, especially if he is conscious of unatoned guilt. "Pierce Thou my flesh with Thy fear: for I am afraid of Thy judgments" (Ps 118:120). "The fear of the Lord is the beginning of wisdom" (Ps 110:10). This holy fear of God is highly important and effective for the work of salvation. It is the indispensable condition of a true philosophy of life; it helps to reawaken and reconstruct the supernatural life of the soul; it is the first rung on the ladder of perfection and the ever-necessary means of safeguarding, strengthening, and perfecting the spiritual life in all its stages.

But these things can never be accomplished by *fear alone,* for fear is an effective means only when accompanied and supported by *hope.* Fear alone may crush the proud spirit of the sinner and wake the careless from their false sense of security; but it will never be able to lift up the human heart, much less to direct it on the way of salvation and to supply it with new vitality. This is done by *hope,* which is rooted in faith and leads to love. Hope encourages the heart that is crushed with fear to seek ways and means of escaping the dread judgment of God and to obtain from His infinite mercy and goodness grace and pardon, sanctification and salvation. This truth is illumined and corroborated in our text. For though the picture of the Last Judgment in the first part of the *Dies Iræ* is purposely designed to inspire fear, the second part brings out in bold relief the penitent sinner's confident hope of pardon. Aside from the special content of the different stanzas, the entire second part gives expression to a cheerful confidence in God by the very fact that it contains a whole series of humble and confident petitions, for which the foundation and motive are not only divine faith but also Christian hope. The prayer of petition has ever been the flower and the fruit of hope—especially of a living, strong, powerful hope.

After the presentation of such dreadfully earnest truths and terrifying motives, we naturally ask: How are these childlike and confident petitions for mercy psychologically justified? We answer: First of all, these truths contain one of the most effective motives for confidence and love, because they point out the great goodness and long-suffering mercy of God, Who does not immediately punish the sinner but gives him time and grace to repent, to do penance, to prepare for judgment, and, thereby, to save his soul (see 2 Pt 3:15). "It was not the avenging justice but rather the merciful love of God that revealed these truths to men—that love which constantly repeats, in a hundred ways, that God wills not the death of the sinner but that he be converted and live."[55] Truly, it is owing to God's mercy "that we are not consumed: because His commiserations have not failed" (Lam 3:22).

Comforting and elevating, moreover, is the thought that the office of the Great Judge will be exercised by Christ according to His human nature, in which He resembles His brethren (see Heb 2:17), in order thus to temper and soften the severity of the sentence.

Finally, there is presented for our contemplation not an exclusive picture of the future judgment of the world, but we are bidden to look back upon the past and to seek comfort, courage, and confidence in meditation on the life, Passion, and death of Jesus Christ. And rightly so, for as long as the "acceptable time," "the day of salvation" (2 Cor 6:2) lasts, Christ is for us not the severe and unrelenting Judge but the merciful Savior. Therefore, it is easy to understand why the soul, which has been mightily stirred by the contemplation of that day of wrath, should melt into tears of sorrow and contrition, which will not cease to flow until the heart and soul of him who pleads is "poured out" before God, Who is the foundation of his hope and his "helper forever" (Ps 61:9; and 41:5). On the Day of Judgment, only those will be saved and summoned by God into His Kingdom who now invoke, fear, and venerate His holy name. "Seek ye the Lord, while He may be found; call upon Him, while He is near" (Is 55:6).

Rex tremendæ maiestatis
Qui salvandos salvas gratis,
Salva me, fons pietatis.

"King of awful majesty, Who freely saves those who are to be saved, save me, O Fountain of Mercy."

The juxtaposition of these two titles of Christ again recalls in one brief sentence the ever-recurring theme of our Sequence. The title "King of awful majesty" is a recapitulation of the first part, which recalled the Second Coming of Christ, in order to awaken and nourish in our hearts a salutary fear of God; the title "Fountain of Mercy" anticipates the second part, which refers to His first coming and is primarily designed to revive and strengthen hope and confidence in the heart of the sinner. The first coming, "when God became man, lived humbly and died lovingly for our sakes,"[56] is perfected and completed by the Second Coming, at which the Lord will call upon all men to render an account of the use or misuse they have made of the graces of redemption. For this reason, the two are usually united, both in Scripture and the sacred liturgy, so that the remembrance of Christ's dreadful and terrifying Second Coming should spur us on to make proper use of His first coming, so rich in graces, so that we can look forward with confidence to His coming as Judge: *præsta, ut Unigenitum tuum, quem Redemptorem læti suscipimus venientem quoque Iudicem securi videamus*; "grant that we, who now with joy receive Thine Only-Begotten Son as our Redeemer, may behold Him without fear when He cometh as our Judge."[57] Both the first and the second coming of Christ partake of the character of a judgment, for both times He comes "for the fall and for the resurrection of many" (Lk 2:34). The work of salvation will be brought to its final perfection at the Last Judgment, when God will admit the just into Heaven and deliver the wicked to eternal torments in hell. The present stanza makes mention only of the redemption or salvation of the "elect" (*salvandi*), which is said to attain its final perfection with the arrival of the "King of awful majesty."

Jesus broadly describes His judgment of the world in the Gospel, and when He speaks of the final sentence, He calls Himself a "king" (Mt 25:34, 40). This title is employed also in our stanza. The judicial power is a natural emanation of royal dignity and rule. To Christ's sphere of kingly activities belong various acts that entered into the foundation, the development, and the consummation of the Kingdom of God among men. The foundation of His Kingdom was performed by Him personally and in a visible manner on earth. The government of it throughout the centuries is the work of His invisible hand through visible organs and representatives. The final act of universal judgment will again be His personal work, for He is to reappear in a visible manner at the end of the world, when He will render unto men, in accordance with their conduct, eternal reward or eternal punishment, and in His now fully perfected Kingdom, will rule forever and ever (*regni eius non erit finis.*) At this most solemn function of the Last Judgment, Christ will manifest and exercise

His kingly power to the fullest extent; He will unfold and reveal all the splendor, beauty, and glory of His heavenly Kingdom. What a dreadful, shocking, and crushing effect this "majesty" of His kingly splendor and judicial glory will have upon the wicked may be gathered from the fact that in the presence of this awful majesty, even the elect will be filled with reverential fear and trembling.

Qui salvandos salvas gratis.

Christ, the all-powerful King, seated on the throne of divine glory, saves His faithful servants out of pure mercy and goodness; in fact, the salvation of men is the work and proof of God's grace. The word *salvare* in this connection has a profound and comprehensive meaning. It signifies the redeeming power of Christ in its fullest and widest application, that is, not merely the deed by which He accomplished the Redemption of man while on earth but also His continued *activity* in Heaven, through which, as Head and Mediator of mankind, He apportions to every individual justice, peace, and eternal happiness. His work and His activity are the ultimate reason of "salvation" for all who were lost through sin. He is truly the "Savior" of men, for He heals them from sin and will free them from the danger, nay, even from the possibility of sinning. He snatches them from eternal perdition and saves them from eternal death. He lavishly dispenses His graces and makes their souls and bodies participants in the fullness of His heavenly glory. "The grace of our Savior Jesus Christ, our Lord and God, frees us from the necessities and evils of our present, miserable life. This is clearly indicated by His very name, Jesus, which signifies that our Lord is our *Redeemer* or *Savior*, especially in this sense, that He will not permit that after this life we shall enter upon another—not another life, but a more miserable and eternal death (*ne post hanc miserior ac sempiterna suscipiat, non vita, sed mors*)."[58] Christ is the author of the supernatural life, the founder and perfecter of salvation; "neither is there salvation in any other" (Acts 4:12). It is only through His saving power and activity that those are redeemed who receive "the inheritance of salvation" (Heb 1:14).

The salvation of the redeemed sinner is an entirely free and unmerited gift of divine love. Justification is given to us freely (*gratis*), that is, as a merciful gift of Christ, as a precious donation of divine forbearance and power (see Rom 3:23–26). "For by grace (*gratia*) you are saved (*salvati*) through faith, and that not of yourselves, for it is the gift of God" (Eph 2:8). It is the power of God that presents us with the greatest and most precious gifts, in a word, with everything that is necessary for supernatural life and participation in the very nature of God (see 2 Pt 1:3–4). As Christ was under no obligation or necessity to redeem us, so on our part there can be no previous merit and, above all, no strict right to Redemption: it is all pure grace, by which we are cleansed and sanctified and thus enabled to win complete and eternal salvation and happiness.

More than that: Redemption comes to us not merely without any merit on our part but in spite of our demerits and our guilt, which has made us "children of wrath" (Eph 2:3) and enemies of God (see Rom 5:10), wholly unworthy of His mercy and grace. The deepest and ultimate reason for our deliverance from the miserable and helpless condition of sinfulness lies in the "great mercy" of our Divine Lord and Savior, Jesus Christ (1 Pt 1:3). "God (Who is rich in mercy), for His exceeding charity wherewith He loved us, even when we were dead in sins, hath quickened us together in Christ (by Whose grace you are saved), and hath raised us up together, and hath made us sit together in the heavenly places, through Christ Jesus. That He might show in the ages to come the abundant riches of His grace, in His bounty towards us in Christ Jesus" (Eph 2:4–7).

The statement that Christ saves the predestined (*salvandi*), i.e., all who actually attain their salvation, and that He does this freely (*gratis*), out of pure mercy, grace, and goodwill, presupposes, of course, that all who attain the use of reason freely cooperate with the graces of Redemption, so that on the Day of Judgment, "the just Judge" will render to them eternal glory, not merely as a gift of mercy but also as a "crown of justice" (2 Tm 4:8). Christ is the first and principal—but not the only—reason of salvation. He does not wish to save men without their cooperation, and if they do not cooperate with His grace, they will be lost through their own fault. Those who are saved, are saved through the grace of Christ; those who are lost, are lost through their own fault.

Salva me, fons pietatis.[59]

If we wish to belong to the number of the elect, therefore, we must zealously walk "in good works" (Eph 2:10). Among these good works, confident appeal to the divine mercy, that is, *prayer*, must be reckoned as the most general means by which everyone can obtain the grace of salvation. Therefore, we now appeal to Jesus—to Jesus Who, since His glorious Resurrection and Ascension, is seated at the right hand of God the Father in heavenly glory. For us, He is not yet the stern, inexorable Judge but the inexhaustible source of heavenly mercy and grace. *Salva me*—that is, save, redeem, beatify me by snatching me, soul and body, from evil and admitting me to heavenly glory. In His excessive goodness and generosity, He will give the humble petitioner more than he deserves or asks for. Jesus is "the mildest and meekest pardoner of our offenses, the most forbearing Judge, full of mercy, Who hides the sentence of His just severity with the merciful cloak of His gracious redemption (*iudicium suæ iustæ severitatis abscondens post miserationem suæ piæ redemptionis*)."[60] For He not merely desires but literally yearns for our salvation.[61]

THE NINTH STANZA

"Save me, redeem me, make me happy, Thou Fount of heavenly mercy."—This prayer, from here till nearly the end of the Sequence, is repeated, amplified, and variegated, always with reference to the basis upon which every appeal for mercy must rest.

Recordare, Iesu pie,
Quod sum causa tuæ viæ:
Ne me perdas illa die!

Fear and hope are the principal emotions which are aroused and stimulated by meditation on "the last things" or on "the eternal truths." Thus far, the emotion of fear has been predominant; but from now on, we find hope springing forth from the heart of the faithful Christian. It is true that he is still mindful of "that day," whose terrifying events have been so vividly and accurately brought home to him, but the picture that now holds him enthralled is not that of the "King of Majesty," the Judge of the World, but rather the vision of the Savior as He lived and taught and acted while on earth; and he calls upon Him with the sweet name, "Jesus," by which the Savior was most familiarly known among men. In order to accentuate the significance of this sweetest and holiest of names, and to impress us more favorably with "the goodness and kindness of God our Savior," Who appeared in the world (Ti 3:4), mention is made of the *gentleness* of Jesus (*Iesu pie*).

With childlike confidence and tender affection, the "loving Savior" is asked to "remember" that He came down from Heaven and spent a long life of suffering from the crib to the Cross in order to save us.

This particular method of meditation, in which the *individual* considers himself and his soul as the object of the Redemption and refers what was done for humanity in a very special

> sense to himself and, as it were, claims it for his own personal benefit, is perfectly justified by the dogma of divine providence (which embraces not only the whole human race, but every individual member thereof), and by its immediateness is well calculated to move the Christian soul powerfully and to fill it with most ardent sentiments of love and gratitude towards God and Christ. At the same time it brings home to the soul the heavy responsibility that weighs upon it if it fails to make the right use of the proffered grace and makes itself utterly unworthy of that grace. We consequently find this method of meditation used quite often and in various forms by the Fathers of the Church and the saints, by Christian pulpit orators and ascetical writers.[62]

"Such is My love," says eternal Wisdom, "that it neither decreases in the individual nor increases in the multitude; I am with you alone at all times, and so deeply concerned about doing all things for you as if there were nothing else in the world for Me to do."[63] Every redeemed sinner may and must, therefore, exclaim in joyful gratitude with St. Paul: "The Son of God ... loved me (*dilexit me*) and delivered Himself for me (*pro me*)" (Gal 2:20).

> O Paul, what are you doing? You claim for yourself what belongs to all, and call the salvation of the whole world your own property. For he does not say, "Who hath loved *us*," but "Who hath loved *me*." And yet the evangelist writes: "God so loved the *world*" (Jn 3:16), and you yourself say: "He spared not even His own Son, but delivered Him up for us all" (Rom 8:32). What does Paul mean? He beholds the hopeless condition of mankind and the incomprehensible solicitude of Christ; he sees the evils from which He has delivered us and the graces He has showered upon us, and,

all aglow with the fire of divine love, he bursts forth in these words. Moreover, he wishes to show that each and every one of us is indebted to Christ in the same way as if He had come for him alone. As a matter of fact, Christ would not have hesitated to accomplish the loving work of redemption for even one single soul, for He loves every human being with infinite love even as He loves the whole world.[64]

Mea est mortalitas nati, mea infirmitas parvuli, mea expiratio crucifixi, mea sepulti dormitio; "Mine is the mortality of the child, Mine is childish weakness, Mine the death of the cross, Mine the sleep of the grave."[65]

If we interpret the word *via* (way, pilgrimage, curriculum) in its restricted, i.e., theological sense, it signifies the life of servitude which began at the moment of Christ's conception and continued till it reached its climax on Calvary, that is, found its profoundest depth and consummation on the Cross. But if we interpret the term in a somewhat wider sense, referring it to Christ's whole life on earth, it includes His burial, His Resurrection, and His Ascension.

In Bethlehem, the Eternal Word comes forth from the undefiled womb of the royal Virgin, as from a bridal chamber in which He had wedded our human nature, and though He was as yet but an Infant wrapped in swaddling-clothes and lying in a manger, the God-Man was nevertheless a true hero, eager and strong, rejoicing "to run the way," to begin and to end His triumphal march (Ps 18:6). At His Incarnation, He came forth from the Father in Heaven and, after having completed His toilsome journey, He returns to the Father at His death (see Jn 16:28); as a dead Man He wished to descend to the dead, for His body was laid in the tomb while His soul descended into limbo (see Eph 4:9) and abided there until the glorious morning of the Resurrection; and then, after a brief interval, He ascended with body and soul to Heaven, to sit in eternal glory at the right hand of the Father. Like a triumphant warrior, He blazed a trail of victory and of grace that began in the heavens above and led to the depths of the grave, and from there back again to "the end of heaven" (Ps 18:7). He was "raised up" before the eyes of His disciples, and "a cloud received Him out of their sight" (Acts 1:9). "This last step concluded the long journey of Jesus Christ upon earth, which had begun in the cave at Bethlehem and led Him to the tomb on Golgotha; from thence He had turned to the Mount of Olives and finally ascended to the portals of Heaven, where the Divine Wanderer at last reached his goal."[66]

For the love of man and for our eternal salvation, the God-Man, during His heroic life upon earth, drank out "of the torrent in the way" (Ps 109:7), a veritable flood of labor, humiliation, and suffering. The most sublime revelation and the most touching proof of His sympathetic and self-sacrificing love for us lies precisely in this, that He freely renounced the perfection and glory of His human nature by "taking the form of a servant" (Phil 2:7), that is, assuming human nature in its weak and lowly state, in order that He might be able to suffer and to die for us. By a unique miracle, He united in Himself the common weaknesses and frailties of human nature (insofar as these were consistent with His dignity and demanded by His mission) with the Beatific Vision of God, which His soul enjoyed from the beginning. Hence, until His death, He was truly a "pilgrim upon earth" (*viator*), though at the same time "blessed" (*comprehensor*). As a consequence, His entire life and work, His unremitting prayers and labors, His bitter suffering and death, were all "redemptive," that is to say, a source of merit and satisfaction for the whole world.

Thus Jesus wished to be our leader on the steep and thorny path of life, and because His heart beat in sympathy with all our needs and miseries, He was truly "a merciful and a faithful Priest before God, that He might be a propitiation for the sins of the people"

(Heb 2:17). "Because with the Lord there is mercy, and with Him plentiful redemption" (Ps 129:7), which the Savior obtained "by His own blood" (Heb 9:12); for this reason, we may confidently call upon Him to save us from eternal "perdition."

Ne me perdas illa die!

"On that day," which is "a day of ... perdition of the ungodly men" (2 Pt 3:7), since the judgment which is then rendered upon all men will condemn the wicked to eternal punishment in hell—on that day "let me not be lost, do not permit me to go to hell." Judas, the traitor, one of the apostles, was lost, and Christ Himself called him a "son of perdition" (Jn 17:12). "In order that His creatures might not become the victims of destruction (*ne perderet, quos condidit*),"[67] the Son of God became man. "For God sent not His Son into the world" to a life of servitude and death on the Cross in order "to judge (*iudicet*: sentence, condemn) the world, but that the world may be saved (*salvetur*) by Him" (John 3:17). "The Son of Man came not to destroy (*perdere*) souls, but to save (*salvare*)" (Lk 9:56).

The two petitions: "Salva me" (save me) and "Ne me perdas" (do not consign me to eternal perdition) are not exactly synonymous, as the first has a much wider meaning than the second. Our Divine Savior desires and effects the salvation (*salus*) of men, but not their destruction (*perditio*); it is only on the supposition of grievous sin, which God simply permits, that He may be said to will eternal damnation as a necessary consequence of, and punishment for, sin; and He gives judicial expression to His will to punish sin by destroying "both soul and body in hell (*perdere in gehennam*)" (Mt 10:28).[68]

THE TENTH STANZA

The life of Christ upon earth, more than our own life, bore the character of a real *journey*; it was truly a wandering in a strange land, a continued pilgrimage to His heavenly home. "Having come from Heaven, He followed His lost sheep upon earth, laid down His life for them, and then ascended again into Heaven."[69] The two most important and significant stages of this journey, namely, Christ's public life and His bitter Passion and death, are given special mention and briefly characterized in the tenth stanza of the *Dies Iræ*:

Quærens me sedisti lassus,
Redemisti crucem passus:
Tantus labor non sit cassus!

Jesus, Who finds it necessary to rest because He is fatigued and weary from the labor of seeking out sinners on the highways and byways of life—what a touching contrast to the picture of Christ seated on the throne of glory to judge the whole world! "For the Son of Man is come to seek (*quærere*) and to save that which was lost" (Lk 19:10). This text admirably expresses the mission of the Redeemer, which is to seek out and to save lost souls, so that all who are willing will find salvation.

The first line of the stanza recalls a *parable* of the Savior and an *event* in His life, both of which admirably characterize the nature and purpose of all His public life. The event referred to is recorded by St. John (see 4:6ff.). Jesus made all His arduous apostolic journeys on foot and, quite often, was completely exhausted from hunger and thirst. On a certain occasion, He arrived at noon, therefore in the hottest part of the day, in the neighborhood of Sichem, and, being "wearied with His journey," seated Himself for a brief rest on the protecting wall of a well that had been built many centuries before by the patriarch Jacob. *Erat ... ibi fons Iacob. Iesus ergo fatigatus ex itinere, sedebat sic supra fontem. Hora erat quasi sexta* (Jn 4:6). Here He sought and awaited a soul that was lost, a woman of Samaria, whom He wished to save. This Samaritan woman is typical of every sinner who is in need of redemption, and typical, therefore, also of the soul that pleads: *Quærens me sedisti lassus*.

This line reminds us also of the consoling parable of the Good Shepherd, Who goes to seek the sheep "which is gone astray," and, when He finds it, "rejoiceth more for that than for the ninety-nine that went not astray" (see Mt 18:12–13; Lk 15:3–8). The sheep that has gone astray is the poor, fallen human race, or, if you prefer, the sinful soul estranged from God. The Good Shepherd, Who sought the lost sheep, is the Son of God. He came into the world to spend Himself in seeking out the poor lost sheep on the rough and thorny desert wastes of life, and lead, nay, carry them back to the green pastures and the protecting fold. His quiet, hidden life, and even more so His public life, His unremitting toil in teaching and working miracles, and finally His sufferings and death—all these were naught else but a seeking after the lost sheep.

This search He continues through all the ages. Christ pursues every soul gently, forgivingly, insistently, until the time of probation is passed and the soul is secure in Heaven. The greater this wearisome search has been, the more He rejoices with His angels over those who are saved. The fullest measure of joy, however, He will experience only after the judgment, when He will gather all the lost but now found sheep into one fold, into the house of His heavenly Father. The whole work of Redemption has its origin in the merciful decree by which God determined that we should become "conformable to the image of His Son," "the firstborn amongst many brethren" (Rom 8:29), that is, in His decision that not "one of these little ones," i.e., those who believe in Jesus, who love and follow Him, shall ever be lost (see Mt 18:14; Jn 10:28–30). As a lost sheep, I wander about in a strange land, in the desert of sin and misery; "hear me, O Lord," and turn me back from the error of my ways, that I may find rest, comfort, and sustenance with Thee; for "I have longed for Thy salvation, O Lord; and Thy law is my meditation" (Ps 118:145, 174). Only if Thou seekest me with Thy prevenient grace and Thy tender mercy, shall I be able to seek Thee also, "and Thy judgments shall help me" (Ps 118:175).

Redemisti crucem passus.

"Thou didst redeem me by Thy passion and death"; for me Thou didst not hesitate to "submit to the torments of the Cross" (*crucis subire tormentum*). This thought, too, is indicated in the parable referred to above, for Jesus, the Good Shepherd, not only seeks His lost sheep to the point of fatigue and exhaustion, but He gives His life for them (see Jn 10:11ff.); He saves and redeems them by "the blood of His Cross" (Col 1:20), by "His Cross and His death (*per crucem et passionem suam*)."[70] *Quid anima non audeat apud tam ambitiosum amatorem? Quid non ab illo speret, qui se quæsivit e cælo, vocavit a finibus terræ? Nec modo quæsivit, sed acquisivit. Adde et de modo acquisitionis in sanguine acquisitoris*; "What may the soul not expect from a Lover Who took upon Himself so great an enterprise? What may she not hope for from Him Who descended from Heaven to seek her? Nor has He only sought her, but has found and made her His own with a great price: that is, the blood of the purchaser."[71] Christ's whole life was "a cross and martyrdom," but especially its final stretch, the *via dolorosa* that grips every sympathetic soul, and, above all, the way of the Cross, that dolorous way of suffering that began with the sentence of Pilate and led to Calvary and the grave. For this reason, the imitation of Christ consists in accepting and carrying the Cross, the sign of sorrow and suffering. That is the royal road of the Cross so strongly recommended by the masters of the spiritual life and the only way that will lead the earthly pilgrim infallibly to his goal.

The example of Christ indicates that the earthly life of His disciples must also be a true way of the Cross, the various stations of which are the successive periods of sorrow and of suffering that fall to the lot of every Christian pilgrim.[72] "Take the cross, therefore, and follow Jesus, and thou shall go into the life everlasting. He hath gone before thee (*præcessit*) bearing His Cross, and died for thee upon the Cross (*mortuus est pro te in cruce*), that thou shouldst likewise bear with Him the Cross of penance and tribulation."[73]

Tantus labor non sit cassus!

"Let not so much labor be wasted!" This stanza, like the two preceding ones, closes with a *petition,* and all three petitions have reference to the same object; they harmonize with and supplement one another. For if the soul of the petitioner were not saved but delivered to the devil, then the incomprehensible sufferings of the Redeemer and the infinitely precious price of Redemption, the blood of Christ, would be in vain *for him.* "Jesus, Who became the way to Heaven for us, was exhausted by His journey on earth. Jesus, Who put an end to our suffering, allowed Himself to be crucified."[74] Consider this well and cooperate zealously with Him, so that His bloody sweat and tears will not be lost for you.

THE ELEVENTH STANZA

We may hope to obtain what we have been asking for so insistently on the day of wrath, namely, to escape eternal perdition and share in the full fruits of Christ's death on the Cross, "the salvation of souls" (1 Pt 1:9), provided we obtain remission and pardon for our sins *now,* while the time of God's good pleasure (Ps 68:14; *tempus beneplaciti*) and the time of mercy (Ps 101:14; *tempus miserendi*) lasts. It follows that this stanza is a logical supplement to what has gone before.

Iuste iudex ultionis,
Donum fac remissionis
Ante diem rationis.

"Just Judge of vengeance, grant me the gift of pardon before the day of accounting dawns." Note the dogmatic exactitude of the expression, *donum remissionis*. The remission of the guilt of sin in the strict and proper meaning of that term can never be merited. It is only in a very broad sense that we can speak of deserving what is and will always remain a free *gift* of God, to which the repenting sinner can never have a legal claim. In like manner, the Church prays for the gift of pardon in one of her Lenten hymns.

Not only in His divine nature but also *as man*, Jesus Christ possesses and exercises the right to pardon and the power to forgive sins. This power, which is essentially divine, He possesses because of *His dignity* and, in His glorified state, also because of the merits of His atonement, by which He not only satisfied for the sins of men but also merited for Himself the power and the right to apply the grace of salvation to the individual soul by means of the forgiveness of sin. But Christ makes use of this power of pardon only in this world; it is only during the days of our earthly probation, only while "the time of visitation" (see Lk 19:44) lasts, that He pardons our sins and remits their punishment. As soon as "the day of accounting" (*dies rationis*) has *dawned*, He will be "the just Judge" (*iustus iudex*) Who "rigidly investigates all things" and Who will leave no good deed unrewarded and no sin unpunished.

The inexorable, impartial justice of the Divine Judge, "Who, without respect of persons, judgeth according to every one's work" (1 Pt 1:17), is sharply emphasized here, and the author points out that at the Last Judgment, the avenging, punishing, wrathful justice of God will be revealed in a special manner. "I begin to take long deep breaths, the light of the world is fading fast, and there comes to me a vision of the other world. What a woeful sight! O God, just Judge in that strictest of judgments, how heavy in the scales of Thy justice appear the insignificant things which no one heeds! Cold sweat and the agony of death are upon me. O angry God, how terrible are Thy judgments!"[75] The severity of His justice is shown primarily by the exactitude with which He will insist on settling our affairs at the particular judgment and the affairs of all men at the general judgment at the end of the world. "Woe unto us in that dread hour, when we shall have to render an account of every idle word, of every wasted moment, of every neglected good deed, and when all the idle words we have ever thought, spoken, or written, in secret or in public, will be made manifest before God and the whole world and will be understood by all."[76] So long as they are on earth and preparing for eternity, the Lord in His generosity pours out upon His children natural talents and goods, as well as the most varied spiritual treasures, the merits and fruits of His Redemption; but a day will come when all will be asked to give an account, even to the smallest detail, of the use or misuse they have made of these God-given talents, of their cooperation with the grace of God, of the use they have made of their time, and of their stewardship of the things that were entrusted to their care. "Every one of us shall render account to God for himself" (Rom 14:12). The greater the graces conferred upon us, the stricter will be the judgment and the reckoning.

> Christ in His unutterable goodness wished to make known to us the manner in which the universal judgment is to be held, in order that we might anticipate it and prepare ourselves for the strict examination and sentence of the Divine Judge ... the severity of the procedure has been revealed to us, in order that we may seek mercy by performing works of

mercy while it is still time. Therefore, let him who expects mercy from Christ, now show mercy to the poor (*misereatur pauperum, qui sibi volunt parcere Christum*).[77]

THE TWELFTH STANZA

Now indeed is the appointed time for mercy and salvation, the time set aside by God for the outpouring of His grace, so that we may be converted and amend our life. *Now* we must seek out and call upon the Lord, we must turn to Him, while He is still inclined to be merciful; only by a genuine, sincere, and effective *penance* may we hope to escape punishment. Heeding the warning of the prophet, we must "be converted with all [our] heart, in fasting, and in weeping, and in mourning" (Jl 2:12).

Ingemisco tamquam reus,
Culpa rubet vultus meus:
Supplicanti parce Deus.

"I groan like a condemned criminal; my face is red with guilt; spare the humble suppliant, O God."

Here we have a description of true contrition, of a genuinely penitential and sorrowful disposition of the soul, not defined in its essential constituents but described in its sensible effects and exterior manifestations. The sighs of the heart, the blushes of shame, and the humble apology all betoken and reveal the genuine spirit of penitence in which they originate. This spirit is essentially one of sorrow and detestation of sin. The contrite sinner regrets and detests the evil of sin, which he himself has deliberately caused. It is true that this detestation and sorrow are rooted primarily and mainly in the *will*, but sometimes they operate so effectively upon the emotions that the guilty sinner breaks forth into groans and sheds tears. Under the weight of his guilt and punishment, the contrite sinner labors in groanings and waters his couch with tears (see Ps 6:7). "I am afflicted and humbled exceedingly: I roared with the groaning of my heart. Lord, all my desire is before Thee, and my groaning is not hidden from Thee" (Ps 37:9–10).

While sighs issue from the heart, which is crushed by the weight of sorrow and sin, the face grows red with the blushes of shame.

Culpa rubet vultus meus.

This is the case especially when hidden sins are disclosed to others or compared to the lesser faults and imperfections of others. St. Ignatius in his Spiritual Exercises proposes as the fruit of the first meditation on sin that we desire and ask God for the grace of "shame and self-abasement," because conversion originates in shame, just as "pride is the beginning of all sin" (Ecclus 10:15). This feeling of shame is salutary, for it "bringeth glory and grace" (Ecclus 4:25) by leading to serious penitence and sincere amendment. Sin is so hideous, disgraceful, and dishonorable that we naturally blush for shame if we have done wrong, in the presence of men and even more so in the presence of the all-holy God. *Commissa mea pavesco et ante te erubesco: dum veneris iudicare, noli me condemnare*; "I dread my misdeeds and blush with shame before Thee: when Thou comest to judgement, condemn me not."[78]

Sincere penitence, contrition, and sorrow necessarily vent themselves in *prayer*, which in turn, naturally takes the form of a plea for forgiveness and mercy.

Supplicanti parce Deus.

Crushed by the burden of sin and keenly conscious of his guilt, the penitent sinner cannot of his own strength amend his life and save his soul, but he is compelled to throw himself upon the tender mercy of Him Who "looketh on the low" (Ps 137:6), and therefore he directs a short, fervent prayer to the Divine Redeemer, Who never rejects a contrite heart. With the deep humility and reverence demanded by the consciousness of his own guilt, as well as by the realization of the dignity and power of the Divine Judge, he begs "to be spared" (*parce*), that is, to be treated with kindness and mercy. He has the disposition and attitude of the publican who, "standing afar off," considered himself fortunate for being allowed to occupy the last place in the Temple, and who, humbly conscious of his guilt, "would not so much as lift up his eyes toward heaven, but struck his breast" as an admission of his guilt and a proof of his contrition, saying: "God, be merciful to me a sinner" (Lk 18:10–14). "This ejaculatory prayer from the heart of the publican has become the canon and model of the prayer for every penitent sinner."[79]

THE THIRTEENTH STANZA

True, supernatural penitence guarantees the remission of all sins—but only when it is combined with "confidence in divine mercy."[80] The knowledge, rooted in faith, of God's infinite majesty, holiness, and justice, and the consideration of the malice of sin and its evil consequences, disturb the sinner and fill him with fear of God's judgments. This fear is wholesome if it is accompanied and borne by the confident *hope* of receiving God's pardon. This hope is indispensable, even more necessary than fear, because the place of the latter in the work of conversion may be taken by the more perfect motive of love. The express and emphatic mention of *hope*, which saves the sinner from despair, lifts up his crushed spirit, and supports him by the infusion of a new, life-giving grace, is therefore eminently proper at this time:

Qui Mariam absolvisti
Et latronem exaudisti
Mihi quoque spem dedisti.

"Thou, Who didst absolve Mary, and didst hear the penitent thief, hast given hope also to me."

In these words, the humble petitioner confesses his guilt and sinfulness and, at the same time, manifests his determination to lay his case confidently into the hands of the Divine Savior in order that he may not fall into the hands of the stern Judge and inexorable Avenger. By word (see the parables) and deed, Jesus Christ during His earthly pilgrimage constantly manifested a truly divine gentleness and benevolence toward sinners who felt their misery and desired to save their soul. Two famous penitents, one a man, the other a woman, both distinguished and encouraging examples of God's unbounded mercy, are now mentioned. Both are examples and models of a sudden yet permanent conversion.

The Roman Church in her liturgy has constantly adhered to the solidly established opinion that Mary Magdalen, Mary, the sister of Lazarus and Martha, and "the sinner" (*peccatrix*) mentioned in Luke 7:37, are one and the same person. Hence, too, Catholics generally know and venerate only one woman by the name of Mary Magdalen, surnamed "the penitent," either tacitly presupposing or expressly asserting the identity of the three Marys. Similarly in this stanza, too, the name "Mary" has reference to the unnamed sinner, that is, to the penitent Magdalen (see Lk 8:2). The complete conversion and transformation of the erstwhile sinner, Mary Magdalen, is one of the most beautiful and touching incidents in the life of our Divine Savior, Who avowedly came "to save that which was lost" (Mt 18:11). Freed through His power from seven evil spirits and attracted by His grace, Mary followed the promptings of a grateful and penitent heart and, heedless of public opinion, hastened to the home of the Pharisee in order to anoint the feet of her Divine Benefactor. By this proof of affection and respect, as well as by the mute appeal of her tears, she desired to confess her guilt to the Master, to express her sorrow, and to ask His forgiveness. The Savior publicly testified that her sins were forgiven "because she hath loved much," reassured her by saying, "Thy sins are forgiven thee (*remittuntur tibi peccata*)," commended her for the faith she had in Him, and then dismissed her "in peace" (Lk 7:47–48, 50). Her perfect love of the Savior drew from His heart and lips the assurance of forgiveness and peace.

Even more remarkable was the equally sudden and complete conversion of the penitent thief upon the cross.

> One of the thieves who were crucified with Christ believed in Christ as the Son of God, was justified, and admitted into Paradise. Who can explain the mystery of so great a grace? Who can describe the power of such a wonderful transformation (*tam miræ commutationis*)? In a moment, the guilt of many sinful years is blotted out: in the midst of his suffering, the agonizing thief, paying the penalty of his crimes on the cross, turns to Christ, and the grace of Christ confers upon him whose malice had incurred punishment the crown of eternal life.[81]

It may be that the penitent thief had previously heard of the teaching and miracles of Jesus, and that what he had heard, and particularly what he now saw, influenced his conduct. But even so, we can explain his sudden and, at the same time, perfect conversion only by the *extraordinary* effect of divine grace. The few words which he spoke to the other thief and to the crucified Savior manifest a truly penitential disposition. Filled with the fear of God, with sorrow and contrition, he publicly and humbly acknowledges, abhors, and confesses his sins and, to atone for them, willingly undergoes the tortures of crucifixion, admitting that he had been justly condemned and received the reward due to his evil deeds. Even more marvelous and extraordinary is his enlightened faith in the absolute innocence and exalted dignity of Christ and his hope and confidence in the royal power and tender mercy of the bleeding, dying, Savior. He shows this when he rebukes the other thief by saying in reference to Christ: "this man hath done no evil," and by his own modest, humble appeal: "Lord, remember me when Thou shalt come into Thy kingdom" (Lk 23:41–42). That this penitential disposition was dictated and perfected by a supernatural love of God is clearly evident from Christ's answer. He forgave him all his sins and assured him of complete pardon by declaring that on "this day" (Good Friday), He would receive him into paradise, i.e., the limbo, that haven of rest and peace where the souls of the Old Testament saints awaited His coming, where he was to see and enjoy the glory of God (Lk 23:43). Tradition gives the good thief the name Dismas and assigns to him a place at the right side of Christ Crucified. Since he was, as it were, beatified by Christ Himself, the Church commemorates him on March 25 or April 24.

The story of the penitent thief is pertinent here not only because it incites and encourages the sinner to do penance but also because it may be applied typically to the Last Judgment. Christ's crucifixion between two thieves "shows more clearly that His Passion and death were undergone for the sins of men, with and for the sinners. The conversion and pardoning of the penitent thief shows the efficacy of the death of Christ and its application to all, even the greatest sinners, provided they are willing to accept His pardon, whereas the impenitence of the other thief indicates that not all sinners will have a share in the graces of the Redemption. Thus Christ's crucifixion between two thieves typifies His relation to the whole of mankind, particularly at the universal judgment."[82] "Jesus Christ, the Son of God, was nailed to the Cross, which He Himself had carried, and with Him were crucified two thieves, one at His right, the other at His left, in order to foreshadow the separation of the good from the wicked at the Last Judgment. The faith of the believing thief typifies the lot of those who will be saved, while the malice of the blaspheming thief illustrates the lot of those who will be condemned."[83]

THE FOURTEENTH STANZA

Preces meæ non sunt dignæ,
Sed tu bonus fac benigne,
Ne perenni cremer igne.

"My prayers are not worthy of being heard; but Thou, Who art good, graciously grant that I may not burn in everlasting fire."

It is characteristic of the prayer of petition that what it asks for is not something the petitioner has deserved, which, therefore, divine justice cannot deny him, but a gratuitous favor expected from God's goodness and generosity. The granting of our petitions, therefore, always is an act of pure kindness, mercy, and condescension on the part of God. This applies particularly to the petitions for mercy addressed to God by penitent sinners. Good works (especially fasting and almsgiving), as well as devotion, humility, confidence, and perseverance, increase the value and power of prayer in the eyes of God. Deeply moved by the sense of his own impotence and sinfulness, the petitioner confesses that his prayers are imperfect, faulty, and unworthy, and that, consequently, they do not deserve to be heard (*preces meæ non sunt dignæ*). Yet the sinner does not despair but rests his hope the more firmly upon the goodness of Him Who alone is entirely and infinitely good, because He is the Supreme Good (see Mk 10:18).

Sed tu bonus fac benigne.

In Holy Scripture and in the sacred liturgy, God's goodness is often emphasized and extolled in order to arouse hope and awaken charity in the hearts of men. *Confitemini Domino, quoniam bonus: quoniam in sæculum misericordia eius* (Ps 105:1; and 117:1).[84] Praise ye the Lord and thank Him, for He is good and kind; His mercy, infinite, inexhaustible, incomprehensible, endureth forever. "Truly, this is the most concise and at the same time succinct expression of divine praise to say that 'the Lord is good,' that 'He alone is good,' and that His 'goodness,' which created, redeemed, supported, protected and sanctified you, is manifested in His inexhaustible mercies."[85] "The Lord is good to them that hope in Him, to the soul that seeketh Him" (Lam 3:25), i.e., in humility, uprightness, and simplicity. *Misericordiæ eius non est numerus et bonitatis infinitus est thesaurus*; "Whose mercies are without number, and the treasure of Whose goodness is infinite."[86] *Proprium Dei est, ut sit bonus*; "It is proper to God, to be good."[87] The Lord is, first of all, infinitely good in Himself, in His *very* essence and will, and as Eternal Love (see 1 Jn 4:8), He is infinitely good also in His external manifestations. His goodness, kindness, benevolence, mercy, mildness, patience, and longanimity are all transcendently great and precious. With full confidence, therefore, the petitioner expects from and asks the infinitely good God, "Whose nature it is always to show mercy and to spare,"[88] to preserve him from the greatest of all misfortunes—the eternal torments of hell.

Ne perenni cremer igne.

The object of the frequently repeated petitions for help is here stated concretely. The line we have just quoted expresses clearly and definitely the most terrible of all dogmas, that of the eternity of hell. To burn with body and soul in everlasting fire, without interruption and alleviation, unendingly, everlastingly in "the furnace of fire" (Mt 13:42), is so cruel and frightful a torture that the mere thought of it fills the soul with consternation. What makes hell such a terrible place is that its punishment is eternal. The unchangeable, endless duration of the pains of hell fills us with horror. Because this dread truth is of great practical importance for the moral life, it is frequently and urgently enforced both in Sacred Scripture and Tradition. "Which of you can dwell with devouring fire? which of you shall dwell with everlasting burning (*cum ardoribus sempiternis*)?" (Is 33:14). The Savior Himself repeatedly emphasizes the everlasting and inextinguishable nature of the fire in which the damned will be tortured and punished (Mt 25:41, *ignis æternus*; Mk 9:42, *ignis inextinguibilis*). Satan and his followers will be cast into the abyss, into the sulphurous burning pool, where "the smoke of their torments shall ascend up forever and ever: neither have they rest day nor night," but are tortured "forever and ever" (Apoc 14:11; 20:10). They shall be ever dying yet never die, and therefore hell is called an eternal death: "death shall feed upon them" (Ps 48:15). Even as the glory of God fills the saints with joy, so the pains of hell torture the damned with eternal bitterness, and they will be filled with eternal despair, for they know full well that their suffering shall never have an end.[89]

The flame of hell, kindled and fed by the breath of God, forever burns and tortures the bodies of the damned, without consuming or destroying them. "Who would not tremble at the mention of these eternal torments? Who would not fear these evils without end (*mala nunquam finienda*)?"[90] The unbelief and forgetfulness of men cannot destroy hell but rather pave the way that leads to it, while, on the other hand, frequent and serious reflection upon these thought-provoking truths is the best safeguard against an unhappy, comfortless, and hopeless eternity. "If the aspect of a corpse makes a powerful impression upon us, how can the thought of the eternal, inextinguishable fire of hell leave us unmoved? If we would always think of hell, we would not easily get into it. It is for this reason that God so often threatens us with the punishments of hell; He would not do so, if the thought of hell were not salutary. Because the thought of hell is able to produce such wonderful effects, God sends it as a preventive medicine, for the soul that fears hell will not easily fall into sin."[91]

THE FIFTEENTH STANZA

The next two stanzas, in their content and partly also in their wording, are taken from Scripture—from the prophetical description of the end of the world and of the Last Judgment, which our Lord Himself drew in bold, clear outline:

Inter oves locum præsta
Et ab hœdis me sequestra
Statuens in parte dextra.

"Appoint me a place amid Thy sheep, separate me from the goats, and place me at Thy right hand."

The separation of the good from the wicked precedes the sentence of the Great Judge. When all nations, all men, all the children of Adam are gathered together before the Son of Man seated upon the throne of His majesty and glory, "He shall separate them one from another, as the shepherd [at evening] separateth the sheep from the goats: and He shall set the sheep on His right hand, but the goats on his left" (Mt 25:32–33).

> The Lord compares the good to *sheep,* meek and tractable creatures; the wicked He compares to *goats,* which are stubborn, perverse, and vicious. Good and bad must be understood in

> reference to the manner of their whole life and particularly of their condition at death. Sheep and goats, though their habits of life are different, form one herd, just as the good dwell together with the wicked in this world; at the end of the world, however, they will be separated according to their deserts, even as the chaff is separated from the wheat, and will remain separated for all eternity. This definite separation and assignment of a position either to the right—the light and favorable side—or to the left—the dark and evil side—marks the eternal fate of every man, the irrevocable sentence of judgment.[92]

That the elect at the Last Judgment are to be separated in space from the sinners seems evident, and almost equally evident is the literal interpretation of the teaching that the elect are to take up their position at the right, the reprobates at the left of the Great Judge. The right side is the favored and more honorable place which logically belongs to the elect. Moreover, the separation indicated has a pertinent symbolical meaning. The right side typifies the happiness and salvation of the elect, while the left side indicates the misery and the everlasting curse that shall rest upon the damned. This view can easily be reconciled with the widespread belief that the transfigured bodies of the elect "shall be taken up ... in the clouds to meet Christ" (1 Thes 4:16), while the hideous, cumbersome bodies of the wicked will grovel in the dust of the earth on the Day of Judgment. This final *separation,* so painful and so humiliating for the wicked, will last forever and ever. Everyone will have assigned to him a definite place according to his merits before God: What will be yours?

> If you wish to be separated from the goats on the Day of Judgment, and to take your place with the sheep, then like a meek lamb follow the guidance of the Good Shepherd now;

be humble, meek, patient, pure; become more and more like the Lamb of God, Who offers Himself daily as a sacrifice upon our altars, and your place will some day be at the right hand of the Eternal Judge, the 'Shepherd of Nations.'[93]

THE SIXTEENTH STANZA

The imposition of the eternal, unchangeable sentence, and the immediate execution of that sentence, will mark the end of the solemn judicial process that will take place at the end of the world.

Confutatis maledictis,
Flammis acribus addictis,
Voca me cum benedictis.

"When the accursed have been confounded and given over to the angry flames, then call me with the blessed."

The judgment of the good and of the wicked is evident even before it is announced: for all who are to obtain eternal life stand assembled at the right hand of the Judge, whereas those who are to be condemned are at His left. When the separation has been duly carried out, then the "King" of majesty, Who has now assumed the sovereign control over all mankind, will "say to them that shall be on His right: Come, ye blessed of My Father, possess you the kingdom prepared for you from the foundations of the world" (Mt 25:34; *Venite, benedicti Patris mei: possidete paratum vobis regnum a constitutione mundi*). "Then He shall say to them also that shall be on His left hand: Depart from Me, you cursed, into everlasting fire, which was prepared for the devil and his angels" (Mt 25:41; *Discedite a me, maledicti, in ignem æternum, qui paratus est diabolo et angelis eius*). This twofold sentence is immediately executed, for "these [the wicked] shall go into everlasting punishment (*in supplicium æternum*), but the just into life everlasting (*in vitam æternam*)" (Mt 25:46). According to the common interpretation, the blessing of the just precedes in point of time the condemnation of the wicked. St. Augustine leaves this question undecided, for the reason that Holy Scripture in various passages seems to follow now the one, now the other order.

Since the measure of reward and punishment varies with the deserts of each individual, the particular judgment will be made known to each by divine illumination; but it is highly probable that Jesus Christ will actually speak the words of blessing and condemnation in a voice ringing with majesty and easily understandable by all.

Confutatis maledictis.

The "accursed" will be so completely convicted by the omniscient and infallible Judge, they will be so beaten down with shame and disgrace, fear and anguish, that they will silently accept their sentence, without an attempt at self-defense or the mention of a mitigating circumstance for their sinful conduct. *Omnis iniquitas oppilabit os suum*; "All iniquity [out of shame] shall stop her mouth" (Ps 106:42). Silence will be imposed upon all evildoers forever. All those who stand at the left side of the Judge are "cursed" (Ps 118:21), "children of malediction" (2 Pt 2:14), perpetually under the curse, subject to the wrath of divine justice. Malediction will be their eternal portion, even as beatitude will be the inheritance of the good (see 1 Pt 3:9). This unhappy state the reprobate sinners have prepared for themselves through their own fault; for "blessing and cursing" were set before them (Dt 30:19), but they loved cursing, and therefore the curse now comes upon them, and they will have nought of blessing. "He put on cursing like a garment, and it went in like water into his entrails, and like oil in his bones; ...

[it became] like a garment which covered him, and like a girdle with which he is girded continually" (Ps 108:18–19). This is the dreadful lot of those who abide not in the words of the Law and fulfill them not in works (see Dt 27:26).

The curse hurled against the wicked includes above all the *loss of God and of Heaven*. They shall be forever separated and banished from the sight of God (see Mt 25:41), eternally cast out from the Kingdom of God into "exterior darkness" (Mt 8:12), eternally excluded from the glorious society of the angels and saints, eternally deprived of all heavenly blessings and joys, particularly of the Beatific Vision of God. To all this must be added the sum-total of the unbearable pains and sufferings of hell, chief among which are the *torture of fire*.

Flammis acribus addictis.

The sentence of the Great Judge will consign the reprobate sinners to the glowing flames—as victims of divine justice condemned to eternal death. In a preceding stanza, the *duration* of hellfire was emphasized; now special emphasis is placed upon its *intensity*, the vehemence of the pain and torture caused by it. The fire of hell is a real fire, substantial and material, a fire that inflames, glows, burns, and gives off smoke, yet no light. Even in this world, there is no element that causes such violent suffering and such terrible tortures as fire: how much more will this be the case of the fire which has been specially prepared by the almighty power of God for the punishment of the wicked! As the joy of Heaven surpasses all the joys of earth, so the tortures of hell exceed every imaginable pain that can be inflicted here below. The sinner must already in this world tremble at the thunderous words of condemnation with which the Great Judge will deliver the damned to eternal fire. The just alone will have nothing to fear from this "evil hearing" (Ps

111:7; *ab auditione mala*), from the judgment of condemnation that will proceed from the mouth of the Judge. "Those that now gladly hear and follow the words of Christ ... shall not then need to dread those words of eternal damnation."[94]

Voca me sum benedictis.

At the right side will stand the elect, called "the blessed of [the] Father" (Mt 25:34), because they owe that perfect, heavenly, eternal blessing which is now their portion to the special favor and love of God, whereas the reprobate sinners must place the blame for their condemnation entirely upon themselves. Inasmuch as the inestimable joys and glories of Heaven come from God and make man truly joyous and happy, they are designated as "blessings." The God and Father of our Lord, Jesus Christ, hath blessed them with spiritual blessings, as He chose them in Him before the foundation of the world, that they should be holy and unspotted in His sight in charity (see Eph 1:3–4). God the Father, according to His great mercy, hath regenerated them unto an incorruptible and undefiled inheritance, which is reserved for them in Heaven (see 1 Pt 1:3–4). Holiness and its eternal reward—the Beatific Vision in Heaven—are a special gift of favor and love by God to His elect. He in His free and gracious providence has called them to be saints, has predestinated, called, justified, and glorified them (see Rom 8:28–30). The saints are, therefore, above all the blessed and beloved children of the heavenly Father.

The humble petitioner desires to be received among "the blessed," to be "called" as they are "called"; for "blessed are they that are called to the marriage supper of the Lamb" (Apoc 19:9; *beati qui ad cœnam nuptiarum Agni vocati sunt*). For while Christ will banish the sinners from His sight and consign them to the "place of torments" (Lk 16:28), the abyss of fire, He *calls* the just with infinite kindness and invites them into the Kingdom of eternal glory. If we wish to hear this blessed call from the mouth of our Judge—at the hour of our death as well as at the general judgment—we must *now* faithfully follow the Savior's call and "labor the more, that by good works [we] may make sure of [our] calling and election" (2 Pt 1:10) for all eternity.

As soon as the Great Judge has pronounced the twofold sentence, it will forthwith be executed. "These [the reprobate sinners] shall go into everlasting punishment, but the just into life everlasting" (Mt 25:46). "With these undoubtedly certain and irrevocably decisive words, in which the eternal, unchangeable destiny of every man is clearly expressed, God will terminate the judgment of the world and disclose to all the vista of eternity—an eternity of reward and joy for the just, of punishment and suffering for the wicked."[95] The dismal abysses of hell will open wide to swallow the damned, and then will close upon them forever, while the hosts of the elect will soar upwards in clouds of light toward the heavenly Jerusalem, into the Paradise of bliss, the Kingdom of light and of peace, to find rest there and to gaze upon, love, and praise the triune God forever and ever. That will be the last and most marvelous, beautiful, and glorious *procession* in which the children of the triumphant Church will participate, and which will end when they enter the portals of their eternal home.

THE SEVENTEENTH STANZA

All of the above-quoted petitions for salvation and admittance to Heaven will be heard and answered on the Day of Judgment only if the petitioner has departed this mortal life in *the state of sanctifying grace*. The moment of death definitively decides his lot for all eternity. It is fitting, therefore, that these petitions conclude with a fervent prayer for that special grace which crowns and secures all others—namely, "the great grace of final perseverance (*magnum illud usque in finem perseverantiæ donum*),"[96] in other words, the grace of a happy death.

Oro supplex et acclinis,
Cor contritum quasi cinis:
Gere curam mei finis.

"Prostrate on my knees I pray, with a heart contrite as though crushed to ashes: Have mercy on me in my last hour."

Since there is question here of a necessary, important, and precious gift, the petitioner seeks both by his outward demeanor and by the interior disposition of his soul to gain favor with the Lord and, as far as possible, to make himself worthy of the desired grace. He humbles himself, bends his knees, prostrates himself upon the earth; he leans on the goodness of God with childlike trust and confidence. The spirit of pride and disobedience has been broken, the heart has melted in the furnace of sorrow and love; it is now reduced to ashes, i.e., it is soft, pliable, and impressionable. Such a heart, humble and contrite, the Lord will not despise but will accept as a pleasing sacrifice.

Gere curam mei finis.

God's wisdom reaches "from end to end mightily, and ordereth all things sweetly" (Ws 8:1). His providence extends over all His creatures. The above-quoted petition, however, has reference not to the all-embracing providence of God but to that special, *loving care* by means of which He guides the elect safely and infallibly to their eternal salvation. This special care, direction, and guidance includes exterior protection and interior graces—but above all a *happy death,* coming at a moment when the soul is in the state of sanctifying grace. Only he who perseveres in grace to the end of his life and dies in this state will be saved (see Mt 24:13). The actual attainment of our final destiny is and will always remain a *special favor of God,* a gift of divine love and mercy, which cannot be merited, in the strict sense, but may and must be asked for by humble, fervent, and persevering prayer. With great calm and confidence, therefore, we lay our worries into the hands of the Lord, for, deeply conscious of our own helplessness and weakness, we unceasingly beg and implore Him, our kind and loving Father, to guide our steps, to straighten our path, to lead, guide, and protect us, to watch over us, and to preserve us from all evil, especially from sin and an evil death. "I am a beggar and poor: the Lord is careful [solicitous as a father] for me" (Ps 39:18; *sollicitus est mei*). He is moved by my misery and desires my salvation. As long as this period of earthly probation lasts, all the redeemed of the Lord, and every individual soul amongst them, are truly "in misery," that is, burdened with the weight of suffering and affliction, with no certainty as to their last end. Only one thing is certain: the Lord "hath care of you" (1 Pt 5:7), and He "delayeth not His promise ... but dealeth patiently for your sake, not willing that any should perish" (2 Pt 3:9).

THE SIX CONCLUDING LINES

Lacrimosa dies illa,
Qua resurget ex favilla
Iudicandus homo reus:
Huic ergo parce Deus.
Pie Jesu Domine,
Dona eis requiem.

Here our Sequence returns to its beginning, that is, to the consideration and representation of the Last Judgment. Terse brevity marks the final description of the terror-inspiring events of this day. "Doleful shall be that day, on which guilty man shall rise from the glowing embers to be judged." It is entirely in line with the dominant color and tone of our Sequence, which was primarily written to arouse and feed the true penitential spirit, that the Day of Judgment should now be called "a day of tears" (*lacrimosa*), just as, in the beginning, it was described as "a day of wrath" and "a day of reckoning." Naturally, this characteristic of the Judgment Day will be the portion only of the reprobate sinner, whose punishment and shame will be further augmented by the resurrection of the body and the publicity of the sentence, now made known to the whole world. In the opinion of those theologians who teach that the destruction of the world by fire will precede the resurrection of the flesh, and that those who are then alive will meet their death in this fire, the description of the guilty "rising from the glowing embers" refers to all men. The text itself does not demand this interpretation. For since the dissolution or disintegration of the body into dust and ashes is the natural and ordinary effect of death, the expression *ex favilla* may have reference not only to the resurrection of the destroyed, disintegrated bodies but also to the resurrection of the dead in general, even if their bodies have not yet suffered corruption. It is the guilt of unrepented, unatoned, and unforgiven sin that makes Judgment Day and the judgment itself an object and source of fear, anguish, and tears. Penance—sincere, earnest, humble penance and a genuine purpose of amendment—alone will enable us "to flee from the wrath to come" (Lk 3:7).

After the humble petitioner has offered so many prayers *for himself,* fraternal charity bids him be mindful of others, living and dead, and his concluding prayer is for them: "Spare him, O merciful Jesus, and grant them eternal rest. Amen." In a previous stanza, the petitioner asked for mercy for himself (*supplicanti parce Deus*); now he repeats his petition for every living, sinful soul. The underlying motive of this prayer is found in the preceding stanza. Because the inexorable Divine Judge will rigidly investigate and pass sentence upon the life of every sinner on that day, a prayer is offered asking Him here and now, as long as the time of mercy and probation lasts, to spare the sinner, that is, to "rebuke [him] not in Thy indignation, nor to chastise [him] in Thy wrath" (Ps 6:2), but to bear with him awhile, give him a chance to repent, save him from the self-occasioned misery of sin, and, finally, keep him from being eternally lost through his own fault.

The very names here given to Christ express both the fullness of His power and the wealth of His mercy. Because Christ, the God-Man, is now glorified and will appear as the Judge, He is called "the Lord" (*Dominus*), a name which clearly indicates His sovereignty and His supremacy in point of dignity and power over all creation. He possesses the fullness of royal and judicial power over all, in particular over all rational creatures, since these are in a special sense His own, totally dependent upon, and eternally subject to, Him. His supreme authority will now, "in the day of thy strength," appear in formidable majesty, all opposition to His Kingdom will be broken, and He Himself, glorious "in the brightness of the saints," will come to judge the world (Ps 109:3). *Pie Jesu*—"merciful Jesus"—this invocation again reminds us of all the love and tenderness of the Divine Heart of Jesus, Who while on earth "went about doing good and healing all that were oppressed" (Acts 10:38). *Revolve Evangelium: ubique Iesum invenies et citum et copiosum ad veniam.*"[97]

The reference to the poor souls in Purgatory in the last verse follows naturally from the use that is made of our Sequence in the liturgy for the dead. "Grant them rest—eternal rest," is the petition that, like a haunting melody, runs through the entire service for the deceased. The poor souls—how they long and sigh for this blessed rest in the heavenly Jerusalem! When "life's fitful fever"[98] on this earthly pilgrimage is o'er, the body rests in the grave: but what does this rest of the body profit the poor, suffering, anguished soul? Her goal is *Heaven*: there alone can she find rest from the worries and labors, the pangs and sufferings of this life. And this it is what we desire and plead for on behalf of the dead—a full and perfect, a heavenly, eternal rest in their true home, which is also ours.

And so this earnest, soul-stirring hymn of penance and sorrow closes with a comforting reference to that rest in God, upon which we are to enter when the days of our earthly labor are ended (see Ps 94:11). The word "rest" exerts a strange spell upon the restless, tired, troubled human heart, which loves rest and seeks it everywhere, but cannot find it anywhere except in God. That which our faith proposes, our hope confirms, and our love accomplishes, is nothing else but *a holy and everlasting rest*, free from care and sorrow. This rest, however, does not consist in idle sloth, but rather in an inexpressible peace of rapturous joy. We rest at the end of our earthly labors by entering upon the joy of the activities of the life beyond. "There indeed we shall rest and see, see and love, love and praise. Behold, at the end of life we shall enter upon a life without end. For what else is our aim and object but to attain to the Kingdom that hath no end?" With these words that illustrious Doctor of the Church, St. Augustine, ends his monumental work, entitled *The City of God*.

ENDNOTES

1 *City of God*, bk. 20, chap. 16.
2 See Augustine, *City of God*, bk. 20, chap. 30, no. 5.
3 John Chrysostom, *Homilies on First Thessalonians*, Homily 9..
4 *Tractates on the Gospel of John*, Tractate 124, no. 5.
5 *Pontificale Romanum*.

6 Jerome, *Commentary on Isaiah*, bk. 14, chap. 51, v. 6.
7 Augustine, *City of God*, bk. 20, chap. 24, no. 1.
8 *Summma Theologiæ*, II-II, q. 172, a. 6.
9 Jerome, *Against Jovinianus*, bk. 1, no. 41.
10 *De Ira Dei*, chap. 23.
11 See *City of God*, bk. 18, chap. 23, no. 1.
12 *City of God*, bk. 18, chap. 47.
13 Augustine, *Tractates on John*, Tractate 7, no. 1.
14 Thomas à Kempis, *Imitation of Christ*, bk. 1, chap. 1.
15 Augustine, *Sermon 311*, no. 14.
16 Augustine, *Expositions on the Psalms*, Exposition on Psalm 103, no. 22.
17 Augustine, *Sermon* 60, no. 7.
18 *Rituale Romanum.*
19 Leo the Great, *Sermon* 9, chap. 2.
20 Cyril of Jerusalem, *Catechetical Lectures*, Lecture 15, chap. 22.
21 See Augustine, *City of God*, bk. 20, chap. 21, no. 2.
22 *Officium Pro Defunctis.*
23 *Pontificale Romanum.*
24 Ibid.
25 Ibid.
26 Denifle.
27 Ambrose, *De Fide Resurrectionis*, no. 114.
28 Augustine, *City of God*, bk. 20, chap. 20, no. 3.
29 Tertullian, *De Resurrectione Carnis*, chap. 1.
30 *Symbolum Nicenum-Constantinopolitano.*
31 Chrysostom, *Homilies on First Corinthians*, Homily 42.
32 Bernard, *In Die S. Pascha serm.*, no. 1.
33 Chrysostom.
34 Bonaventure, *Brevil.*, pt. 7, chap. 5.
35 Tertullian, *De Resurr. Carn.*, chap. 52.
36 *Symbolum Athanasium.*
37 *Officium Pro Defunctis.*
38 *City of God*, bk. 22, chap. 21.
39 Bishop Schneider, *Das andere Leben*, 3rd ed., p. 334.
40 Augustine, *City of God*, bk. 20, chap. 14.
41 Ibid.; *in ea quippe quodam modo legitur, quidquid ea faciente recolitur.*
42 *Symbolum Athanasium*, emphasis added.
43 Leo the Great, *Fifth Homily for Lent.*
44 Augustine, *City of God*, bk. 20, chap. 2.

45 Augustine, *City of God*, chap. 19, no. 4.
46 Leo the Great, *Sermon* 9, chap. 2.
47 Kempis, *Imitation*, bk. 1, chap. 24.
48 *Little Office of the Holy Angels*
49 Thomas à Kempis, *Imitation of Christ*, bk. 1, chap. 24.
50 Tauler.
51 Laurent.
52 Kempis, *Imitation*, bk. 1, chap. 25.
53 Leo the Great, *Sermon* 43, chap. 3.
54 Kempis, *Imitation*, bk. 1, chap. 24.
55 Jungmann.
56 Ruysbroek.
57 *Missale Romanum*.
58 Augustine, *City of God*, bk. 22, chap. 22, no. 4.
59 *Sabbato quodam, dum Cantaretur Sequentia: 'Mane prima Sabbati,' in illo versu: 'Ut fons summæ pietatis,' cogitabat B. Mechtildis, quot et qualia dona inenarrabilia de ipso fonte omnium bonorum emanassent et sine fine emanant. Et ait Dominus ad eam: 'Veni et vide minimum, qui est in cœlo, et tunc poteris cognoscere fontem pietatis.' ... Sic fontem pietatis cognovit in minimo; quia si Deus talia operatus in eo, qui nil boni peregit, quid in virtuosis Sanctis suis perficiet?* (Mechtildis, *Liber special grat.*, pt. 1, chap. 33).
60 *Pontificale Romanum*.
61 *"Avarus est Deus salutis nostræ" (Augustine, Expositions, Exposition 99, no. 10). "Contremisco totus, tuam, Domine Jesu, quantillo possum intuitu considerans majestatem, praesertim cum recordor, in quantis ipsius aliquando contemptor exstiterim. Sed et nunc, cum iam a facie maiestatis fugi ad genua pietatis, quid amplius facio? Vereor ne qui aliquando contrarius exstiti maiestati, et nunc ingratus pietati inveniar.* (Bernard, *Tract. de Mor. et Offic.* Episc., chap. 5, no. 23).
62 Hundhausen, on 1 Pt 1:20.
63 Henry Suso.
64 John Chrysostom.
65 Bernard, *Serm. in Cant.*, 75, no. 7.
66 Laurent, *Christological Sermons*, 1, 652.
67 Sedulius.
68 *Quisquis septem canonicarum horarum officia quotidiana Deo devotione persolverit, si a gravibus criminibus omnimodo alienus, a levibus quoque, inquantum humana fragilitas patitur, cum Dei subvenientis auxilio temperavit, ab his, quae cavere non potest, ut confidenter dicam, in examine tremendi iudicii absolutus erit, et quia*

nunc Creatori suo non negligit iniuncta suae servitutis obsequia reddere, tunc libera conscienta cum b. David atque alacri poterit voce cantare: Septies in die laudem dixi tibi, Domine Deus meus, ne perdas me (Ps 118).—St. Peter Damian, *Opusc. De Horis Canon*, chap. 5.

69 Laurent.

70 Litany of the Saints.

71 Bernard, *Serm. in Cant.*, 68, no. 4.

72 See Oswald, *Eschatologie*, 240.

73 Kempis, *Imitation*, bk. 2, chap. 12.

74 Augustine.

75 Henry Suso.

76 Ibid.

77 Leo the Great, *Sermon* 9, chap. 2.

78 *Officium Defunctorum*.

79 Laurent.

80 Council of Trent, Session 14, "Doctrine on the Sacrament of Penance," chap. 4.

81 Leo the Great, *Sermon* 55, chap. 3.

82 Scheeben.

83 *Cum et salvandorum figuram fides credentis latronis exprimeret et damnandorum formam blasphemantis impietas prænotaret.* (Leo the Great, *Serm. de Passione Dom.*, 4, chap. 1).

84 *Non potuit laus Dei brevius explicari quam ut diceretur: quoniam bonus est. Quid sit grandius ista brevitate non video, cum sit proprium Deo quod bonus est.* (Augustine, *Expositions*, Exposition on Psalm 117, no. 2).

85 P. Wolter on Ps 117.

86 *Missale Romanum*.

87 Ambrose, *Sermon on Psalm 118*, chap. 9, no. 15.

88 *Missale Romanum*.

89 See Ruysbroek.

90 Leo the Great, *Sermon* 9, chap. 2.

91 Chrysostom, *Homilies on Second Thessalonians*, Homily 2.

92 Laurent.

93 Deharbe.

94 Kempis, *Imitation*, bk. 2, chap. 12.

95 Laurent.

96 Council of Trent, *Session* 6, Can. 16.

97 Bernard, *Serm. in Cant.*, 33, no. 4.

98 Shakespeare, Macbeth 3.2.

APPENDIX

Dies Iræ Formal Equivalence English Translation

<table>
<tr><td>Dies iræ, dies illa:
Solvet sæclum in favilla
Teste David cum Sibylla.</td><td>The day of wrath, that day,
will dissolve the world in ashes:
the testimony of David and the
Sibyl.</td></tr>
<tr><td>Quantus tremor est futurus,
Quando iudex est venturus,
Cuncta stricte discussurus!</td><td>How great will be the quaking,
when the Judge is about to come,
strictly investigating all things!</td></tr>
<tr><td>Tuba mirum spargens sonum
per sepulchra regionum,
Coget omnes ante thronum.</td><td>The trumpet, spreading a
wondrous sound
through the sepulchres of the
regions,
will summon all before the throne.</td></tr>
<tr><td>Mors stupebit et natura
Cum resurget creatura
Iudicanti responsura.</td><td>Death and Nature will marvel,
when the creature rises again
to respond to the Judge.</td></tr>
<tr><td>Liber scriptus proferetur,
In quo totum continetur,
Unde mundus iudicetur.</td><td>The inscribed book will be
brought forth,
in which all is contained,
from which the world shall be
judged.</td></tr>
</table>

DIES IRÆ

Iudex ergo cum sedebit,
Quidquid latet, apparebit:
Nil inultum remanebit.

When therefore the Judge is seated,
whatever lies hidden will appear;
nothing will remain unpunished.

Quid sum, miser, tunc dicturus,
Quem patronum rogaturus,
Cum vix iustus sit securus?

What then shall I, poor wretch, say?
Which patron shall I entreat,
when even the just are hardly secure?

Rex tremendæ maiestatis,
Qui salvandos salvas gratis,
Salva me, fons pietatis.

King of tremendous majesty,
Who gladly savest those fit to be saved,
save me, O font of mercy.

Recordare, Iesu pie,
Quod sum causa tuæ viæ:
Ne me perdas illa die!

Remember, sweet Jesus,
that I am the cause of Thy sojourn:
lose me not in that day!

Quærens me, sedisti lassus,
Redemisti crucem passus:
Tantus labor non sit cassus!

Seeking me, Thou didst rest, weary;
Thou didst redeem me, suffering the Cross
let not such labor be in vain!

Iuste iudex ultionis,
Donum fac remissionis
Ante diem rationis.

Just Judge of vengeance,
make a gift of remission
before the day of reckoning.

Ingemisco tamquam reus,
Culpa rubet vultus meus:
Supplicanti parce Deus.

I sigh, as the guilty one:
my face reddens in guilt:
spare the imploring one, O God.

Qui Mariam absolvisti
Et latronem exaudisti,
Mihi quoque spem dedisti.

Thou Who didst absolve Mary,
and heard the thief,
gave hope to me also.

Preces meæ non sunt dignæ, Sed tu bonus fac benigne, Ne perenni cremer igne.	My prayers are not worthy: but Tho Who art good, graciously grant that I be not consumed in eternal fire.
Inter oves locum præsta Et ab hœdis me sequestra, Statuens in parte dextra.	Grant me a place among the sheep, and take me out from among the goats, setting me on Thy right hand.
Confutatis maledictis, Flammis acribus addictis, Voca me cum benedictis.	Once evildoers have been silenced, consigned to acrid flames, call me, together with the blessed.
Oro supplex et acclinis, Cor contritum quasi cinis: Gere curam mei finis.	I pray Thee, beseeching and kneeling, my heart crushed as cinders: Take care of my final end.
Lacrimosa dies illa, Qua resurget ex favilla Iudicandus homo reus:	Tearful, that day, when from glowing embers will arise the guilty man to be judged:
Huic ergo parce Deus. Pie Iesu Domine, Dona eis requiem. Amen.	Then spare him, O God. Merciful Lord Jesus, grant them rest. Amen.

Our mission is to publish authentically Catholic books that are traditional, accessible, and beautiful.

Benedictus Books takes its name from the opening Latin phrase of the Canticle of Zechariah, prayed daily in the Catholic Church since the earliest centuries. Our logo evokes the antiquity of Gregorian chant and the illuminated manuscript tradition, emphasizing continuity with the faith and worship of the past and the continuing relevance of our sacred patrimony today.

Benedictus Books was established in 2021 with the launch of our acclaimed periodical *Benedictus*, the "Traditional Catholic Companion"—a daily devotional drawing on the theological riches and customs of the ancient Roman Rite, and allowing for a deeper experience of the traditional Latin Mass, liturgical calendar, and writings of countless saints and theologians. This periodical reflects the three core values of Benedictus Books:

Traditional. We are committed to preserving and handing on the Faith of our forefathers without diminution or change, publishing works that are both inspired by and conformable to traditional Catholic doctrine, liturgy, and spirituality. Our primary focus is on republishing reliably orthodox works that help to promote the interior life and sanctification of the domestic church through classical forms of prayer and worship.

Accessible. Recognizing that many aspects of Catholic doctrine, liturgy, and custom have become obscured in recent decades, we place an emphasis on texts that explain and assist readers in mining the vast theological wealth that is contained and expressed in the traditional Roman Rite, as well as those writings of saints and scholars that have been profoundly shaped by the same.

Beautiful. Rooted in the perennial tradition of Western sacred art, we believe that texts treating such exalted subjects deserve a truly beautiful and durable presentation. We invest extensive time and meticulous care to create inspiring new typesettings with rich ornament and illustration, crisp typography, clean layouts, and classic bindings to make every book as pleasing to hold and look at as it is to read.

In order to be worthy of the noble content they contain, all of our books are crafted to the most exacting standards, allowing these priceless treasures from our Catholic tradition to be cherished for years to come.